CLASSICS
OF
SEA POWER

The Classics of Sea Power series makes key works of professional naval thought readily available in uniform, authoritative editions. Each book is chosen for its eloquence, incisiveness, and pertinence to the great ideas of naval theory, strategy, tactics, operations, and logistics. The series is a companion to histories, anthologies, and other interpretative writings, providing a depth of understanding that cannot be had from reading secondary sources alone.

Rear Admiral J. C. Wylie was the first serving naval officer since Mahan and Luce to become known for his writings on strategy and theory. *Military Strategy* is a reaction to questions raised in the 1950s during the debate on unification of the U.S. armed forces. In it Wylie attempts to break down deep-seated service parochialism with a comprehensive approach to strategy.

Another of his purposes was to ensure that sea power and maritime strategy were thoroughly appreciated. But Wylie also knew the limits of navies, and was quick to say that sea power is always applied with an eye on events ashore. Similarly, he was both appreciative and critical of air-power and land-power advocates. He was ahead of his time in seeing that guerrilla warfare was a fourth major element of strategic theory. Now, in a personal postscript for this edition, he adds a fifth component, the strategy of terrorism.

Wylie's general theory of power, centered on the sturdy concept of control as its end and developed with an original exposition of cumulative and sequential strategies, is as useful today as when he wrote.

SERIES EDITORS

John B. Hattendorf
Naval War College
Newport, Rhode Island

Wayne P. Hughes, Jr.
Naval Postgraduate School
Monterey, California

Military Strategy

Rear Admiral J. C. Wylie as a captain in command of the heavy cruiser USS Macon *(CA-132) on 30 June 1959 during the opening of the St. Lawrence Seaway. (Bill Ray,* Life *Magazine © Time Inc.)*

J. C. WYLIE, REAR ADMIRAL, USN

Military Strategy: A General Theory of Power Control

With an Introduction by
John B. Hattendorf

And a Postcript by
J. C. Wylie

NAVAL INSTITUTE PRESS   Annapolis, Maryland

Library of Congress Cataloging-in-Publication Data

Wylie, J. C. (Joseph Caldwell), 1911–
    Military strategy : a general theory of power control / J. C. Wylie ; with an introduction by John B. Hattendorf and a postscript by J. C. Wylie.
        p.   cm. — (Classics of sea power)
    Reprint with a new introd. and postscript. Originally published: New Brunswick, N.J. : Rutgers University Press, 1967.
    Includes bibliographical references and index.
    ISBN 0-87021-362-8
    1. Strategy. 2. Naval strategy. I. Title. II. Series.
U162.W9   1989   89-12140
355'.02—dc20   CIP

Series design by Moira M. Megargee

Printed in the United States of America on acid-free paper ♾

CONTENTS

INTRODUCTION

REAR ADMIRAL J. C. WYLIE is a rarity among American naval officers. He was the first serving officer since Luce and Mahan, half a century before him, to become known for writing about military and naval theory. First and foremost Wylie was a sailor, a sea officer, and an accomplished shiphandler, but at the same time he became a careful thinker about strategy.

Wylie came to be interested in abstract theory gradually, through experience and observation during his naval career.[1] Wylie's book, *Military Strategy: A General Theory of Power Control,* was clearly a product of his experience and his professional development as a naval officer. Looking back over his career, one can find in it the ideas and thought processes that led him to write the book. The key influences on his thought came first through an appreciation of cultural differences, which he obtained in his early years with the Asiatic Fleet. This was followed by his combat experience in the Sec-

1. Except where noted, this outline of Wylie's intellectual development is based on the Navy Office of Information biographical sketch of Rear Admiral J. C. Wylie, Jr., dated 22 August 1972, supplemented by the U.S. Naval Institute Oral History, conducted by Paul Stillwell, 21–22 May 1985; Naval War College Oral History No. 7, conducted by Dr. Evelyn Cherpak, 21 November 1985–5 February 1986; and information supplied by Admiral Wylie.

ond World War, his role in the development of the Combat Information Center, and his postwar experience with ergonomics. The stimulation and the time for reflection that he had at the Naval War College during the period when the U.S. Navy was struggling through the bureaucratic battles of service unification were also important elements of his development. All of the separate influences combined to bear fruit through his work with the strategy and sea power study group at the Naval War College in the 1950s. These were Wylie's intellectual steps that led to *Military Strategy*.

Wylie's father, Joseph Caldwell Wylie, Sr., had been graduated from Clemson College in his home state of South Carolina. He went to the New York City area to engage in business, rising to become vice president, secretary, and a director of the Lovell-Dressel Company, manufacturers of marine lighting and signaling equipment.[2] He and his wife had three children, first a son and then two daughters. The boy, named for his father but known as "Bill," was born in Newark, New Jersey, on 20 March 1911 and grew up in Newark and the neighboring town of Glen Ridge.

Reminiscing about his childhood, Wylie was fond of saying "I am a high school dropout who never went to college," because he never graduated from high school and in his day the U.S. Naval Academy did not award an academic degree. In January 1928 he left Barringer High School in Newark, New Jersey, for several weeks to attend Werntz's preparatory course in Annapolis. Upon its completion, Wylie returned home and took a competitive examination offered by his congressman. This examination was also the academy's entrance exam, and through scoring the highest, he earned his appointment. After receiving news of his appointment to the

2. Obituary: J. Caldwell Wylie, the *New York Times*, 16 January 1958, p. 29:4.

academy in April, Wylie left high school before his graduation and spent the remainder of that spring sailing on Barnegat Bay, where his parents had a summer home and where he had learned to love sailing and the sea from an early age.

Having just turned seventeen, Wylie was younger than most of the other midshipmen who entered the academy that summer. In the years that followed, he did well at Annapolis. As *The Lucky Bag* commented in his final year, "Academics have never bothered him. At any rate he always stays well above the 3.0 mark with plenty of time to read all the good magazines and books. . . ." His main extracurricular activity was rowing. "When he found out he was too light for the Varsity and too heavy for the Lightweights, he set his eye on crew managership and attained that difficult position after months of hard work."[3]

Upon receiving his commission in June 1932, Wylie got his orders to the heavy cruiser USS *Augusta* (CA-31). The ship had entered service only eighteen months earlier, and Wylie joined her shortly before she sailed to become flagship of the U.S. Asiatic Fleet. In his first four years on board the *Augusta*, Wylie saw his initial service as an officer in circumstances different from those in other parts of the navy. A small force, the Asiatic Fleet operated as a separate entity, reporting directly to the Navy Department and not through the commander in chief of the U.S. Fleet, as did other major commands. Its primary purpose was diplomatic. Should war break out, the small Asiatic Fleet was to be augmented by the much larger U.S. Pacific Fleet. Thus, the time that the flagship spent on competitive fleet exercises was limited. In Wylie's time, exercises usually took place in January and February each year, leaving the ship free to cruise in a fairly well-established pattern: a few weeks in Hong Kong, visits to ports such as Amoy

3. *The Lucky Bag of the Service: the Annual of the Regiment of Midshipmen* (U.S. Naval Academy: Annapolis, 1932), p. 248.

and Foochow along the China coast up to the mouth of the Yangtze, occasionally up the river as far as Nanking, then north to Tsingtao as a base for the three summer months. In the autumn, the flagship cruised south to spend the winter in the Philippines. During the winter, there were cruises to Singapore, the Netherlands East Indies, and, in 1934, a visit to Australia.

The most dramatic event that influenced Wylie's appreciation of differing cultural perceptions occurred in the summer of 1934. Admiral Frank B. Upham, the commander in chief of the Asiatic Fleet, broke the usual pattern of routine visits and sailed in the *Augusta* from Tsingtao to Yokohama in order to represent the United States at the funeral of Admiral of the Fleet Heihachiro Togo, the Japanese admiral who had defeated the Russian Fleet at Tsushima in 1905. Protocol required that the ship send a platoon of forty bluejackets and two officers to march in the parade. Captain Chester Nimitz decided not to use the regular landing force, and he mustered a special detail of men, all of whom were over six feet tall. Wylie was the ensign, marching along behind the American contingent. Ahead of them were the Japanese and the British. Along the long line of march with the casket and the detachments from many countries, Wylie could hear whispered comments from the spectators, noting that the Americans were a head and a half taller than anyone else in the parade.

When Wylie was ashore in those years, he had an experience of exotic cultures, but one in which two cultures operated in different spheres, each by its own standards. On board ship, Wylie found that the Asiatic Fleet's mission gave service with it a different tone than one found elsewhere in the U.S. Navy. The frequent and conscious connection of fleet operations with diplomacy and international relations made its impact, although the emphasis was on professional naval duties. In this, his first practical experience was guided by a series of very successful officers. His first three commanding officers in the *Augusta* were Captains James O. Richardson, Royal E. Ingersoll, and Chester W. Nimitz, each to rise to admiral within a decade.

In May 1936, at the end of his tour of duty in the *Augusta*, the Bureau of Navigation ordered Wylie to the destroyer *Reid* (DD-369), then under construction at the Federal Shipbuilding and Dry Dock Company in Kearney, New Jersey. The *Reid's* commanding officer was Robert B. Carney, another future chief of naval operations. Thinking back over those years, Wylie exclaimed, "You wonder I thought it was a good navy?"

While he was serving in the *Reid,* he became engaged to Harriette Bahney, daughter of Mr. and Mrs. Luther W. Bahney of Elizabeth, New Jersey. She was a graduate of St. Margaret's School in Waterbury, Connecticut, and the Connecticut College for Women. The couple married on 27 November 1937; they had two children, Elizabeth and Peter, both of whom eventually became naval officers.[4]

After six years at sea, Wylie was transferred to the destroyer tender USS *Altair* (AD-11), based at San Diego. Serving as the ship's communications officer, he remained in her from July 1938 until June 1939, after which he returned to Annapolis for shore duty in the Executive Department at the Naval Academy. In July 1941 Wylie reported to the USS *Bristol* (DD-453), lead ship in a new group of 1,700-ton destroyers built under the "Two-Ocean Navy" Act of 1940. When Wylie reported on board, she was then fitting out for her commissioning at Kearney. During her first year at sea, Wylie participated in patrol and convoy operations in the North Atlantic between Canada and Ireland. The *Bristol's* commanding officer occasionally served as senior escort commander with Canadian, Free French, and Polish corvettes in company.

4. "Harriette Bahney to Wed," the *New York Times,* 10 October 1937, sec. vi, p. 4:7; "Harriette Bahney Wed to Navy Man," the *New York Times,* 28 November 1937, sec. vi, p. 5:1.

In May 1942 Wylie was ordered back to the shipyard at Kearney, this time to be executive officer of the USS *Fletcher* (DD-445), the lead ship in a new class of 2,100-ton destroyers, under the command of William M. Cole. Commissioned in June 1942, the *Fletcher* sailed from the East Coast, arriving at Noumea, New Caledonia, in October, and immediately began patrol and escort duties for the Guadalcanal operation. She bombarded Lunga Point on 30 October, covered reinforcements landing on Guadalcanal on 9 November, and helped to drive off heavy enemy air attacks on the transport ships on 12 November in the first phase of the battle of Guadalcanal.

The *Fletcher* played an important role in the night action off Guadalcanal on Friday, 13 November, firing her guns and torpedoes in the general action that sank two Japanese destroyers and damaged the battleship *Hiei*. Amazingly, the *Fletcher* received only slight damage in the intense battle which, a Naval Academy history textbook notes, "for confusion and fury is scarcely paralleled in naval history."[5] Despite the superior number of Japanese ships and the loss of eight U.S. ships, the Americans forced the Japanese battle force and transports to return to their base. After the action, the *Fletcher* sailed eastward for Espiritu Santo in the New Hebrides Islands to refuel and rearm.

On 30 November she put to sea with Task Force 67, a force of cruisers and destroyers, to intercept Japanese ships in another attempt to bring troops to reinforce their positions on Guadalcanal. The *Fletcher* led the American formation westward through the Lengo Channel into Iron Bottom Sound and approached the westerly end of Guadalcanal's north coast. Taking advantage of the latest surface search radar with a Plan Position Indicator display, the *Fletcher* was the first to

5. E. B. Potter and C. W. Nimitz. eds., *Sea Power: A Naval History* (New York: Prentice Hall, 1960), p. 704.

make radar contact with the Japanese off Tassafaronga Point, just before midnight, and to pass on recommendations to Rear Admiral Carleton Wright, the officer in tactical command. Wright, hesitating to use the new technical capability that the *Fletcher*'s radar offered, lost his opportunity as the Japanese seized the initiative. Hampered by faulty exploders and depth-control mechanisms, not one of the American torpedoes found its mark, although one destroyer was sunk by gunfire. The Japanese sank one of the American ships and severely damaged three others.

Wylie was awarded the Silver Star Medal for "gallantry and intrepidity in action" as the *Fletcher*'s executive officer during the two actions off Guadalcanal. "Using discriminating judgement and quick resourcefulness," the citation reads, "Lieutenant Commander Wylie directed the ship, gun and torpedo control of his vessel with outstanding success, inflicting heavy damage on two enemy cruisers and sinking a third. . . ."

During these actions, Wylie's battle station was in the ship's chart house, just abaft the bridge, where he operated the surface search radar. Knowing better than the newly trained radar operators what sort of information the captain needed to correlate the radar information for the best offensive use of the guns and torpedoes, Wylie could talk to the captain through a louvered light screen in the porthole between the bridge and the chart room. While watching the radar scope, he wore split sound-powered telephones, one to the gunnery officer and the other to the torpedo officer. Close at hand, he had a microphone to use the TBS voice radio. It was a jury-rigged arrangement, radical in the light of current doctrine, yet as one historian has commented, "Thus, Wylie was himself the Navy's first Combat Information Center, or CIC, a concept and term that had yet to be invented."[6]

6. Eric Hammel, *Guadalcanal: Decision at Sea* (New York: Crown, 1988), p. 253.

In January 1943 Wylie took command of his first ship, the USS *Trever* (DMS-16), a First World War flush-deck destroyer converted into a fast minesweeper. The *Trever* received the Navy Unit Commendation for her action in the Solomon Islands campaign, which at that point involved little minesweeping and was devoted to carrying troops from Guadalcanal up the Slot for clandestine rubber-boat landings at night.

After only six months in command, Wylie was unexpectedly ordered to Pearl Harbor for duty on the staff of Rear Admiral M. S. Tisdale, commander, destroyers, Pacific Fleet. Wylie was angry that he had been ordered ashore after so short a time in his first command. Tisdale promised him a new command, but explained that the fleet had a higher priority. Tisdale saw the urgent need for commanding officers to use and to correlate the rapidly increasing quantity of information that was becoming available to ships. Impressed by the *Fletcher*'s action report on the Guadalcanal operation, the staff in Pearl Harbor believed that Wylie might be the right man to help in quickly reaching to the heart of the issue. At Pearl Harbor, the question was not merely one of radar and sonar information, but also of air and surface scouting reports, electronic and code-breaking intelligence, and basic navigational and piloting data.

Joining others on the staff who were dealing with this same problem, including Commander Caleb B. Laning and Lieutenant Commanders Edward Day, George Phillips and Lieutenant (j.g.) Robert E. Bookman, Wylie got the job of preparing a short handbook. Within two months he produced the text for the *CIC Handbook for Destroyers*. The destroyer tender at Pearl Harbor printed the first run of about five hundred copies for all Pacific Fleet destroyers and their staffs. It was an immediate success and within a short time was widely reprinted and distributed throughout the navy.

The basic concept that Wylie and his colleagues developed was more than just the thought of having a space and the equipment aboard ship with which to deal with the vast expansion of available information. Their original concept included an arrangement of positions and equipment to correlate the data most profitably. They devised a general plan that could be adapted to whatever ship would use it, basing it on a hypothetical square compartment. Dividing the square compartment in half with a fore and aft line, they assigned the starboard side to air action, or in the case of destroyers at that time, air defense. The port side was devoted to surface and subsurface action. Having established this division, they divided the square compartment the other way, from side to side. The forward half was allocated to "history," anything that preceded the current situation, while "current events" was assigned to the after half.

Using this basic concept, the Destroyer Force staff placed the surface search radar in the after port side for surface current events and recommended that the sonar control console be placed there also. In the forward port side they located the Dead Reckoning Tracer, which showed where the ships and its targets had been. On the starboard side they placed the air search radar in the after portion for "current events," and the air plotting boards forward with "history." They called the officer who controlled all this the "evaluator." His station was between the two radars, within reach of sonar control, where he could see both radar screens and both surface and air plots.

After outlining the basic idea of the arrangement, Wylie and his colleagues went on to work out the duties and responsibilities of the team who would operate the equipment, keep the plots, and man the radios and sound-powered telephone circuits. The Pacific Fleet Destroyer Force staff wanted to call this new coordinating center the Combat Operations Center.

This suggested name did not sit well with the destroyer captains of the day, who could not imagine a captain anywhere but on the bridge. Thus the name Combat Information Center came into use in the U.S. Navy.

Upon the CIC Handbook's completion, Admiral Tisdale sent Wylie to muster support for the *Handbook* at the Bureau of Ships in Washington and the staff of Rear Admiral M. L. Deyo, commander, Destroyer Force, Atlantic Fleet. Despite some opposition from the staff of the commander in chief, U.S. Fleet, Deyo accepted the *Handbook* and the two force commanders agreed to unified requirements. The Bureau of Ships approved the remodeling of the commodore's cabin into a CIC, while the ships' captains were given a Pullman-type roomette arrangement in their sea cabins.

Returning to the Pacific, Wylie went to Espiritu Santo in the late summer of 1943 to start a combat indoctrination school for newly arriving destroyers. Nicknamed "Cocoanut College" because it was located in a cocoanut grove on Aore Island, it was not a formal school in the strict sense. Instead, it was composed of a team of five or six officers who had been in recent combat and could teach officers and leading petty officers the latest ideas based on experience with using the PPI radar scope and coordinating information during combat. The most difficult task they faced was to change ingrained patterns of thought and teach people to solve relative motion problems with their own ship at the center of the plot, rather than the guide of the formation—a key task if the U.S. Navy was to use the new PPI radar scopes effectively.

In December 1943 Wylie left the Pacific and returned to Kearney to take command of a destroyer under construction, the USS *Ault* (DD-698). Through his long experience with that shipyard, Wylie had developed a close relationship with yard workers, and some of those that he had worked with in outfitting the *Reid, Bristol,* and *Fletcher* had now become foremen. This personal connection made for good relations with the yard and high quality in outfitting the ship.

The *Ault* was commissioned on 31 May 1944, and after a shakedown period, Wylie returned with her to the Pacific. As flagship for Destroyer Squadron 62, she sailed from Pearl Harbor to join Task Force 38 at the end of 1944. Beginning in January 1945, the *Ault* entered combat operations. Providing screening, plane guard, and shore bombardment duties, she participated in the Formosa Raids on 3–4, 9, 15 and 21 January; the China Coast Raids on 12 and 16 January; the Nansei Shoto raid on 22 January; the Iwo Jima operation from 15 February to 5 March; the Fifth Fleet raid on Honshu and Nansei Shoto from 15 to 16 February and 25 February to 1 March; and the Okinawa operation from 17 March to 30 May. In connection with the first carrier raids on Tokyo in mid-February and early March, the *Ault* participated as a radar picket for the "delousing" destroyers, providing anti-aircraft fire against Japanese planes that followed the raiders back to the fleet.

Detached from command of the *Ault* in July, Wylie was assigned to duty in Washington, where he reported to Commodore Arleigh Burke in the Special Defense Section on the staff of the commander in chief, U.S. Fleet. This group under Burke's direction had the duty to develop countermeasures to the Japanese kamikazes in preparation for the planned invasions of Kyushu and Honshu. The war ended in August before the group had developed a plan, and it was disbanded.

During the general demobilization of U.S. forces, Wylie served with the Office of Naval Research as a special project officer. Based at Beavertail in Jamestown, Rhode Island, Wylie was project officer for a group of experimental psychologists from Johns Hopkins University, and a number of other academics who had subcontracted with Johns Hopkins, in studies to develop the most efficient control mechanisms for a naval officer to use in controlling complex machinery. Eventually they produced a handbook that could be used by design engineers in developing airplane cockpits and other key control positions. This publication on "human engineering" was an early contribution to what is now referred to as ergonomics, that aspect of technology concerned with the study of problems relating to the mutual adjustment of men and machines.

In June 1948 Wylie reported to the Naval War College as a student in the Strategy and Tactics Course. Toward the end of his year there, he and five or six of his colleagues had a discussion about the navy's situation in the unification of the armed forces. All agreed that what the navy needed most, in order to avoid being sunk in unification, was a clear and succinct understanding of the reason for its existence. They could see that the navy's leaders were not stating any rationale for the navy's role. As the discussion broke up, the students agreed that the first of them to return to Newport on the staff of the Naval War College would try to make some kind of study that could create an intellectually sound rationale for a modern navy.

After Wylie left Newport in 1949 to serve as staff operations officer for Rear Admiral John Higgins, commander, Destroyer Flotilla One, based at San Diego, Admiral Richard L. Conolly received orders to be president of the Naval War College. He had been a student and a staff member in Newport from 1929 to 1931, had extensive experience afloat as a destroyer squadron and amphibious commander during World War II, and in the postwar years had been deputy chief of naval operations for operations. Since 1946 he had been based in London while serving as commander in chief, U.S. Naval Forces, Eastern Atlantic and Mediterranean. Conolly had his own strong ideas about naval strategy and saw clearly the need for new work in this area.[7]

By chance, Wylie received orders to return to the Naval War College as the staff member for the Advanced Course in Strategy and Sea Power in the summer of 1950, just as war began in Korea. Some weeks after Conolly's arrival in Newport in December 1950, Wylie had the opportunity to speak at length with him and discuss his idea for a study of the navy's reason for existence. The idea was very much in tune with Conolly's views, and he instantly seized on a name: the School of Advanced Study in Strategy and Sea Power. This became one of the major efforts in Conolly's initial recommendations for change in the Naval War College curriculum.

By 1 May 1951 Conolly had completed his letter recommending changes to Admiral Forrest Sherman, the chief of naval operations. Incorporating many of Wylie's thoughts, Conolly proposed to extend the usefulness of the Naval War College. Conolly wrote, "While the primary function of the Naval War College must remain the education of naval leaders in command, strategy, tactics, logistics and staff work, its mission is incomplete and unfilled if it does not generate progressive ideas, foster creative thinking in its own field of education and produce an accumulation of knowledge and understanding of the basic elements of the 'Art and Science of Naval Warfare.'" To achieve this, Conolly proposed to establish a Research and Analysis Department as well as the School for Advanced Study. Noting that nowhere in the navy's curriculum was there an opportunity "for a mature, adult appreciation of the orderly intellectual processes evolved for the

7. For a summary of his ideas, see Donald G. White, "Admiral Richard L. Conolly: A Perspective on His Notions of Strategy," *Naval War College Review,* November 1971, pp. 73–79, and Oral History: Columbia University Oral History Program.

study and solution of problems in the social and physical sciences," he went on to declare that the lack of understanding of the naval profession and general lack of intellectual discipline had been convincingly demonstrated in recent years. Summarizing his view of the situation, he wrote:

> . . . we are, as naval officers today, a breed of fine seamen, of able airmen, efficient administrators, and of superb tacticians and technicians. But very few of us, until the forces of naked power stared the nation in the face, were able to reason with the Congress or present our case convincingly to the people so that our own service should be saved from comparative oblivion. Our understanding and our exposition of the indispensable character of our profession and the undiminished and vital nature of Sea Power have been dangerously superficial and elementary.[8]

In this proposal, Conolly and Wylie saw the importance of history. Wylie, in particular, seized upon the suggestion that Admiral Raymond Spruance had made some years earlier to establish a civilian chair of history at the Naval War College. This position had been approved by the secretary of the navy in 1948, but for lack of funds it had never been filled. Wylie saw the importance of history for broad understanding of strategy. Conolly incorporated Wylie's ideas on this subject in his letter to the chief of naval operations:

> All of us have, at one time or another, uttered or acquiesced in the cliché that we learn from history. But few, if any, of us know any history; and none of us now has the time or inducement to study any history on other than a desultory catch-as-catch-can basis. Very few of us have even come to realize that there are three types of knowledge to be had from military history. One is simple knowledge of events that took place; the

8. Naval War College Archives, Records of the Course of Advanced Study: President, Naval War College, letter to Chief of Naval Operations, A3-1 serial 2354-51, 1 May 1951.

second is a knowledge of how to fight better; and the third (and generally neglected) is a knowledge of how to think more clearly in order to properly analyze the situations and assess and evaluate the various factors that produce success or failure, victory or defeat.

Emphasizing his point, Conolly wrote, "In this connection, it should be noted that the history we need is a rather unknown, little understood, facet of the broad chronology. It is interpretative history and there have not been very many interpretive historians who have chosen our profession as their field of study."[9]

Although Wylie was unhappy with Conolly's choice for the name of the course, since it seemed to imply a course that was superior to the other resident courses rather than one that was merely different, he acquiesced. The chief of naval operations approved Conolly's suggestions in July 1951 and Wylie was given responsibility for its administration.[10] At Wylie's request, he obtained as his assistant Lieutenant Commander Eugene Burdick, later to become famous as the coauthor of the novel *The Ugly American*. Together they laid the groundwork for the new course.[11] In the process they consulted a number of university professors, including Harold Sprout of Princeton, Edward M. Earle of the Institute for Advanced Study, William Reitzel of the Brookings Institution, Robert G. Albion of Harvard, and James Phinney Baxter of Williams College. All made useful contributions, but on reflection Wylie found that the advice they had received from John von Neumann of the Institute for Advanced Study and Harold Lasswell at Yale proved to be most influential.

9. *Loc. cit.*: J. C. Wylie, Memorandum [for the President, Naval War College], Subj: Chair of Military History, 2 April 1951.
10. *Loc. cit.*: CNO to President, Naval War College, Op-03 serial 130P03, 3 July 1951; J. C. Wylie, Memorandum for Admiral Conolly, 1245, 5 July 1951.
11. On this, see Wylie's postscript to this volume.

Wylie designed the work to be that of a study group, rather than a course. The early structured part was a means of preparing group members for the primary purpose of their work, which was to be research, study, and the increase of basic knowledge.

In the fall of 1951, after the first group of eight officers had arrived, Burdick began the course with a study of intellectual methods. In actuality this was an appreciation of some of the basic concepts of philosophy and logic.

This approach paralleled a course in maritime history for the period 1500–1900, which was taught on a part-time basis by Professor Thomas C. Mendenhall of Yale University. The purpose of his course was to examine not the usual chronological pattern but the relationship of maritime matters to events in other fields of human activity—the political, social, economic, and cultural. Mendenhall concluded his course with a two-day session in which the group attempted to define the role of contemporary sea power in the light of their historical studies. In this, Mendenhall was the first to serve as the college's professor of maritime history. In the following year he was succeeded by Professor John H. Kemble of Pomona College, who held the position in 1953 as its first full-time occupant when it was named the Ernest J. King Chair of Maritime History. At the same time, the Naval War College established the Chester W. Nimitz Chair of Social and Political Philosophy. These were the Naval War College's first civilian academic chairs.

To sharpen themselves, each member of Wylie's group wrote a weekly paper and then defended it in a seminar meeting in which invited guests could participate. The guests ranged from members of the War College staff, such as Vice Admiral Conolly and retired Rear Admiral Henry E. Eccles, to outside experts, such as Captain Basil Liddell Hart, Dr. Herbert Rosinski, Professor John Masland of Dartmouth College, and Vice Admiral Friedrich Ruge, who in 1956 as

Inspekteur der Marine became the first head of the Federal German Navy.

During this first year, Wylie published some of his own work in connection with the study course. He delivered "Reflections on the War in the Pacific" first as a lecture at the Naval War College in November 1951 while he and his colleagues were examining the historical context of maritime strategy. It was much more than a personal reflection on a segment of the war in which he had a great interest; Wylie took seven events in the war and looked at them as matters that could be usefully studied for reference in improving the strategic conduct of a future war. Considering the use of strategy in the light of his Naval War College discussions of theory and logic, Wylie laid part of the groundwork for his later book, *Military Strategy.*

Most significantly, he developed an idea that had been suggested by Dr. Herbert Rosinski in conversations during the spring of 1951. At that time, Rosinski had tried to identify two different types of strategy: "directive" and "cumulative." Wylie went on to develop Rosinski's ideas further and classified them as "sequential" and "cumulative" strategies. This point was an important one for his later work.[12] Wylie submitted his article to the U.S. Naval Institute, where it earned an honorable mention in that year's prize essay contest and was published in *Proceedings* the following spring.

Following this work, Wylie began during the latter part of the first year to develop his first general statement of maritime strategy. He organized it into an essay that was discussed in the seminar group and then given as a lecture to the Naval War College students on 11–12 September 1952. This, too, he submitted to the Naval Institute, where he again won an honorable mention and publication in *Proceedings* under the

12. The key excerpt from this essay appears as Appendix A in this volume.

title "On Maritime Strategy." Clearly demonstrating the results of his first year's work, Wylie explored the subject in terms of theory, past experience, complicating current factors, and finally, the contemporary use of military and naval power. His ideas on maritime strategy are very briefly summarized in *Military Strategy* and show their basis in this work.[13] Most important, Wylie focused on the idea of control as the aim of warfare. He argued that the division of strategy by service, into maritime, continental, and air strategies was artificial and should be made only for the purpose of study and analysis. "In practice there is, and must be, a good deal of overlap and merging," he wrote. The most important part of this article was Wylie's development of the idea that the purpose of sea power is to project control over the land. In this, he noted, there are two methods:

> a victory by a sea power exploiting her power at sea to project a frequently smaller but strategically decisive ground force for the actual establishment of control on land; and a victory by a sea power exploiting her power at sea to project an economic force toward the eventual establishment of governing control over the enemy in his own land.

"It should be noted that, in practice," Wylie went on to say, "the exploitation of sea power is usually a combination of general slow stiflings with a few critical thrusts. These latter are frequently spectacular and draw our attention to the exclusion of the former, while in point of fact the critical thrusts would not be critical were it not for the tedious and constant tightening of the screws that makes them possible."

In the second year, each member of the group selected a subject for research and defended it in rigorous seminars. As the year wore on, the students decided what they wanted to do with the results of their work. They knew that while few in

13. Reprinted as Appendix B in this volume.

the navy took the time to ponder the abstract statements in professional and academic journals, naval officers did listen to what their senior officers were saying and read their operational orders carefully. Therefore, the group decided that the most influential way in which to get their ideas across was to write speeches for senior officers in Washington and to contribute phrases and paragraphs to fleet operation plans and basic orders. In this way, many of the basic ideas that Wylie and his study group developed received widespread currency in the 1950s and 1960s, penetrating all levels of the service and being borrowed by writers of speeches and operation plans.

While this work was in progress, Wylie published a small piece that revealed the value he placed on the use of careful terminology in discussing strategy. In the spring of 1953, as the study group completed its second year, the navy was doing very badly in the budget hearings in Congress. One of the army's most effective and persuasive advocates repeatedly replied to difficult questions by saying, "Mr. Congressman, that is a calculated risk." Since no one knew what the phrase meant and no one in Congress wanted to gamble on a risk that was not carefully calculated, Wylie teasingly devised a mathematical expression of the phrase in a one-page article for *Proceedings*. Wylie wrote about this formula:

> For the victor it will add a rare quality of intellectual brilliance to his assured rank of major or minor genius. To the unfortunate victim-of-circumstances-beyond-his-control it offers dignified justification. The critics will be so involved in recalculation that their audiences will soon give up in sheer boredom. The ones who were already in accord with the victim's decision will have long since understood it anyway.[14]

14. J. C. Wylie, "The Calculation of Risk," Naval Institute *Proceedings*, vol. 79, no. 7 (July 1953), p. 725.

A commentator, Walter Millis, picked up on Wylie's piece and wrote a column on it in the *New York Herald Tribune* that summer. As Wylie later commented, "The result was that no one ever mentioned the calculation of risk before Congress again for at least five years. So it did serve its purpose."

Before Wylie left the Naval War College in the summer of 1953, he reflected on the course and his suggestions for its future. Among them was a point that guided his own thinking:

> Rather than rediscovery of the areas of continental, maritime and air strategies, use these as a point of departure in appreciation of the problem of the study of strategy. Introduce at this time in the spring term other known or suggested methods of studying or analyzing strategy such as by means of the so called principles, by situational analyses, by other theoretical divisions such as sequential and cumulative classifications, by the doctrinal approach, and by that odd but prevalent joining of faith and osmosis down a path toward a hoped-for understanding.[15]

Concluding his recommendations, Wylie wrote:

> I can not too strongly state my belief that study of this nature is the primary hope for a continued and expanded contribution of the navy to the nation. We can count with reasonable surety on the technical and industrial strength of the nation and its reflection in the technical improvement of the navy. For a better understanding of when, where, and how to apply these technical advances we can turn to no one outside the service. For that deeper understanding of the nature of our profession only we can help ourselves.[16]

In July 1953 Wylie took command of the attack transport USS *Arneb* (AKA-56). It was while in command of the *Arneb*

---

15. Naval War College Archives, Staff File: J. C. Wylie, Memorandum to the President [Naval War College], Subj: Conduct of the Course in Advanced Strategy and Sea Power, 9 June 1953.
16. Ibid.

during long passages at sea that Wylie wrote the basis for what, fourteen years later, was to become his book *Military Strategy*. In 1954 he joined the staff of Rear Admiral H. Page Smith, commander, Amphibious Group Two, as operations officer and later as chief of staff. The next year he was ordered to duty in the Office of the Chief of Naval Operations. During this tour of duty in Washington he had the opportunity to see the navy budget process at work and to observe naval officers as they defended the navy's role. As he watched officers from the other services and listened to their logic, he saw that the naval officers reflected a different manner of thinking than the others. He took this topic as the subject for another article in *Proceedings* entitled "Why a Sailor Thinks Like a Sailor." [17] In October 1958 he took command of the heavy cruiser USS *Macon* (CA-132). Command of this ship marked a high point in Wylie's career. During his period of command, he took the *Macon* through the St. Lawrence Seaway for the opening ceremonies and continued on through the Great Lakes to Chicago, the first (and still the only) cruiser to make such a trip. "Taking a ship the size of *Macon* halfway across a continent was probably the most exhilarating experience that a cruiser captain could ever hope for," Wylie wrote. [18]

From November 1959 to December 1960, Wylie served on the staff of Admiral Robert L. Dennison, the supreme allied commander, Atlantic. Selected for rear admiral during this period, Wylie was promoted on 1 December when he took command of Cruiser Division Three (later renamed Cruiser-Destroyer Flotilla Nine). Wylie was appointed deputy inspector general of the navy in November 1961 and remained in that position until August 1962, when he was assigned to the Joint Strategic Survey Council of the Joint Chiefs of Staff. For

17. Reprinted in this volume as Appendix C.
18. J. C. Wylie, "The Freshwater Cruise of USS *Macon*," U.S. Naval Institute *Proceedings*, vol. 86, no. 4 (April 1960), p. 61.

his service in that position between 1962 and 1964, he was award the Joint Service Commendation Medal.

In July 1964, Wylie reported as deputy chief of staff and deputy chief of staff for plans and operations to Admiral H. P. Smith, the commander in chief, U.S. Atlantic Fleet. He was awarded the Legion of Merit "for . . . outstanding service . . . during Operation Power Pack in the Dominican Republic crisis in April and May 1965. . . . [He] provided invaluable assistance to the Commander in Chief United States Atlantic Fleet during a period when rapid, decisive planning and execution of joint military operations in the Dominican Republic were of the utmost importance to our national interests."

In March 1966 he became deputy commander in chief, U.S. Naval Forces, Europe, and chief of staff to Admiral James S. Thach, the commander in chief, U.S. Naval Forces, Europe. Wylie was serving in this position when his book, *Military Strategy,* was first published by Rutgers University Press.

Completing his assignment in London, Wylie became chief of staff to Vice Admiral John T. Hayward, the president of the Naval War College, and he remained in that position for a year, until he became commander of the Naval Base, Newport, Rhode Island. After only three months he took up the additional responsibilities of the commandant of the First Naval District, with headquarters in Boston, Massachusetts, and with further duty as commander of the naval base, Boston.

Rear Admiral J. C. Wylie retired from active duty on 1 July 1972, after more than forty-four years in uniform. Upon his retirement, he received a Gold Star in lieu of a second Legion of Merit for meritorious conduct as commandant of the First Naval District.

In 1974, following the translation of a series of articles that had appeared during 1972 in *Morskoi Sbornik* by Admiral of the Fleet of the Soviet Union Sergei Gorshkov, Wylie was one of eleven prominent U.S. flag officers invited by the Naval Institute to comment upon Gorshkov's work as it appeared in monthly installments of *Proceedings*. Wylie took Gorshkov's piece on *Analysis of Navies in the Second World War"* for comment, and noted that through this series, "We have gotten a glimpse of a very important mind at work. We should profit by it." [19]

Upon his retirement, Wylie and his wife moved to Portsmouth, Rhode Island. Admiral Wylie remained active, starting work on an analysis of strategy in terms of its historical development. In addition, he served as the first chairman of the USS *Constitution* Museum Foundation, an organization established to provide support for a museum that opened in 1976 in a restored machinery building for the 1832 drydock in the Boston Navy Yard.

At the same time, in the autumn of 1972, he became the first chairman of the American Sail Training Association, which in June 1976 brought 102 sail-training ships to a race from Bermuda to Newport, Rhode Island, in connection with the celebration of the bicentennial of American independence. He retired from these activities in the late 1970s, but has remained an active member of the New York Yacht Club, the Ida Lewis Yacht Club, the Navy Sailing Association, the Coaster's Harbor Navy Yacht Club, the Newport Reading Room, and Quindecim.

Wylie wrote *Military Strategy* while he was in command of the USS *Arneb* in 1953, but he did not submit it for publication until 1966. After expanding and revising the book during those years, Wylie eventually submitted it under the title *The Military Mind* to Rutgers University Press, which had recently published a number of books on military subjects.

---

19. The series was later collected in book form: Sergei Gorshkov, *Red Star Rising at Sea* (Annapolis: Naval Institute Press, 1978). Wylie's contribution may be found following Part 9 on pages 110–111.

They agreed to publish it as *Military Strategy*. The editor suggested the new title so that libraries could more easily index it by its subject.

On 17 April 1967, Rutgers University Press published 2,500 copies of the 111-page *Military Strategy* at four dollars a copy. In recommending the book, *The Library Journal*'s reviewer commented, "Although the price is slightly high for such a small book, the relevance of the topic to today's unstable world and Admiral Wylie's thoughtful discussion of it makes the book essential reading for public and academic libraries."[20]

Reviewing the book for *The New York Times Book Review*, defense correspondent Hanson Baldwin noted:

> No military service can long remain effective without searching self-criticism and continuous re-examination of its own ideas. . . . Wylie, well known in the Navy, is a refreshingly outspoken and thoughtful individual, thoroughly at home on the bridge of a ship, but equally at home in the semantics of dialectical discussion. He has produced a simple but relevant little work in an attempt to promote order in the discussion of strategy.[21]

Shortly after the book appeared, Rear Admiral Henry E. Eccles prepared a review in which he summarized Wylie's main arguments. "On the staff of the Naval War College and in his other assignments, he demonstrated his imagination and his independence of mind in a continuing challenge of conventional assumptions and routine formulations," Eccles noted. "It is a tribute to his dedication that while serving in demanding high-level positions, he was able to produce even

20. K. G. Madison in *The Library Journal*, vol. 92 (May 15, 1967), p. 1930, quoted in *Book Review Digest 1967*, p. 1430.
21. *New York Times Book Review*, November 5, 1967, p. 62.

a short reflective and imaginative work." [22] Eccles pointed out
the debt that Wylie owed to Dr. Herbert Rosinski in developing the analytical classification of sequential and cumulative
strategies. Interestingly, he also pointed out a similarity with
that of André Beaufre's *Introduction to Strategy*. Although
Wylie's work predated that of Beaufre, Eccles found a harmony of thought that "is the natural, if not frequently expressed, result of the combination of hard practical experience in combat command, responsible high-level planning,
innate scholarly bent, a receptive speculative mind and a dis-
satisfaction with mediocrity." [23]

In 1968, Wylie's move to the Naval War College as chief
of staff to Vice Admiral John T. Hayward prompted several
other reviews. Most prominent among them was by Neil
Ulman in *The Wall Street Journal*. [24] "No attempt to proclaim
the last word on warfare," Ulman wrote, "it is a fine introduction to strategic thought and chiefly fascinating as the
forging of a thinker's tool." Underscoring Wylie's point that
the service-oriented theories of strategies create barriers between their proponents and make it more difficult for them to
understand one another, Ulman found Wylie's general theory
of strategy "a very broad statement of strategy, but worth a
book to develop if the power of Admiral Wylie's arguments
can wean planners from hitherto parochial outlooks to a
broader, more flexible approach." In concluding his review,
Ulman wrote that Wylie "clears much of the irrelevant debris
from the foundations of strategic thought and offers planners
a logical point of departure."

22. Naval Historical Collection, Naval War College; Manuscript Collection 52, box 7, folder 15: Papers of H. E. Eccles, Enclosure to Henry E.
Eccles letter to Wylie, 27 March 1967.
23. Ibid.
24. "The Bookshelf: Flexible Strategy," the *Wall Street Journal*, 10 July
1968.

Among readers of strategic theory, Wylie's book became well known. By 1970, Rutgers University Press had exhausted the initial printing. The press reprinted the book in 1970, 1972, and 1977, each time printing 1,500 additional copies. In 1978 the Escuela de Guerra Naval in Buenos Aires, Argentina, translated the book into Spanish. Rutgers sold rights to Greenwood Press in 1980 for a clothbound edition, and in 1987 to the Australian Naval Institute in Sydney for a paperback edition.

Commenting on the Australian edition, Professor Peter Nailor of the Royal Naval College, Greenwich, wrote:

> The book itself was first published in 1967, and it is fair to say that it never received the attention it might have done. The American strategic community was then preoccupied with more specific issues than general theories of strategy; and the reflective cast of the argument—and its brevity, perhaps—somehow eluded the general notice. Nevertheless, the book has many virtues, which are not out of place today, and it is good to be reminded of Wylie's professionalism and clarity.

While the book did not receive widespread attention in the larger defense community, it did have a major role within the navy. As Nailor commented, "Wylie has many claims to be thought of as an intellectual influence upon military, specifically naval, staff thinking."

In the 1980s, as leaders and staff officers within the navy were developing the U.S. Navy's maritime strategy, Wylie's book had an impact on their approach. Some of the staff officers dealing with the detailed development of the maritime strategy were deeply influenced by his ideas and tried to apply his concepts of control, cumulative, and sequential strategy in their work. One of the active participants, Captain Peter M. Swartz, USN, wrote about one of Wylie's essays that it was "by the Navy's leading public strategist of the 1950s and 60s.

Remarkably similar to the views expressed in the Maritime Strategy a generation later."[25]

As the United States Navy moves toward the last decade of the twentieth century, it has come to focus more explicitly on the question of national strategy and the role of the navy within it. Along with this has come renewed emphasis on joint operations and cooperation among the services. In dealing with these matters, Wylie's basic analysis and his statement of a general theory of strategy stand as a clear and eloquent statement from which innovative thought may proceed.

JOHN B. HATTENDORF

25. "Addendum to 'Contemporary U.S. Naval Strategy: A Bibliography,'" p. 53, published in April 1987 as an addendum to the "Maritime Strategy Supplement," U.S. Naval Institute *Proceedings*, January 1986. For a detailed discussion of Swartz's role, see John B. Hattendorf, "The Evolution of the Maritime Strategy: 1977–1987," *Naval War College Review*, Summer 1988, pp. 7–28.

Military Strategy

PREFACE

A FEW YEARS AGO Field Marshal Montgomery visited General Eisenhower at Gettysburg, and the occasion was made newsworthy by Montgomery's criticism of the conduct of the battle that had taken place there nearly a hundred years earlier. The notable oddity in this incident was that the criticism was offered by a professional rather than an amateur.

But Field Marshal Montgomery's criticism was no better, or no worse, than that of the thousands of other critics of that or any other war; essentially all strategic comment or strategic criticism is an *ad hoc* sort of business, having not much more than personal judgment, or hunch, or emotion, or bias, or sometimes even self-interest behind it. The only advantage the professional seems to have over the amateur is a little personal experience, and it is seldom that anyone questions whether or not the personal experience is actually relevant.

I do not criticize the amateur strategist. On the contrary, I believe deeply that strategy is everybody's business. Too many lives are at stake for us not to recognize strategy as a legitimate and important public concern. But what I do decry is that strategy, which so clearly affects the course of society, is such a disorganized, undisciplined intellectual activity. And I believe this state of affairs might be improved.

1

What I have tried to do in this short book is to indicate why I think our existing methods of thinking about strategy are superficial and inadequate, to set forth in bare outline the existing theories of strategy and their limitations, and then to speculate on a general theory of strategy that could provide a basis for more orderly and productive strategic thought than has generally prevailed in the past.

Neither the general theory that I propose nor any better alternate that someone else might propose can guarantee successful strategy any more than a good political theory can guarantee successful government. But a theory can provide a stable and orderly point of departure from which we might proceed to the specific facts at hand in devising, in carrying out, and in later criticizing a strategy for a particular purpose.

There is more work to be done, a great deal of it, before we can force order into situations inherently disorderly, before we can better predict the inherently unpredictable, and before we can apply equivalent experience to situations inherently novel in the vast social and technological revolutions of our time. In view of the urgent weights of the many separate parts of these social and technological revolutions, perhaps the most important thing a valid general theory of strategy might do is to ensure that our interest in the trees does not blind us to the forest.

I do not know whether my speculations on strategic theory will turn out to be valid—obviously I think they will or I would not offer them—but now that they are in print, the next move is up to someone else. And if this short book manages to induce someone else either to refine and amend what I offer, or to propose something different and better, then it will have served a useful purpose.

It goes, almost without saying, that the opinions or assertions in this discussion are mine and are not to be construed as official or as reflecting the views of the Navy Department, the naval service at large, or the Department of Defense.

J. C. WYLIE

London
September, 1966

CONTENTS

CHAPTER ONE

THE MILITARY MIND AND STRATEGY

T HE MILITARY MIND is, of course, a catch phrase. For a
good many years it has been used to suggest a pedantic,
rather dull, professional soldier who was either monumentally
stupid or unbelievably wrong about one thing or another. It
was a caricature that was only occasionally accurate. Fortunately, there are not very many of him, not nearly so many,
I sometimes suspect, as of his cousins in some of the other
professions. This Colonel Blimp does not actually exist in
great numbers, and where he does he is seldom important.

But there do exist some very real military minds, both individually and collectively, and the products of those minds will
sooner or later, as they have in the past, have a profound
effect on our nation and on our society and its civilization. It
is a premise of this discussion that we do not know nearly as
much about the military mind as we do about a good many of
the others, and a corollary that we do not know nearly as
much as we usefully might.

The political minds of men, for instance, have for a good
many centuries been subject to intense and continuing study
and analysis. The effects of those minds at work, and the
effects of the study of those political minds, have had a considerable influence on the course of human events. The influence of Locke on Jefferson, or the influence of Pareto on Mussolini, or the influence of Jefferson or Rousseau or Mussolini

or Winston Churchill on other men's lives, is too well recognized to need comment.

The economic minds of men are similarly dissected and analyzed and interpreted by literally thousands of men, both formally in the universities and informally but no less astutely by economic practitioners of all descriptions in their own daily lives. Their interest lies in why economic man thinks as he does, which is, in effect, why he acts as he does. And if you doubt that economic ideas can have much effect on economic practice, just reflect a moment on the effect of Adam Smith or Marx or Keynes or Henry Ford on the world we live in today.

So, too, in other fields of human activities. All the great areas of the social process have evolved some sort of an orderly, disciplined study whose aim is understanding why and how men think as they do, and why and how they act as they do within one or another of those general areas. In all of them, that is, save one. It comes as something of a surprise to realize that of all these huge areas of mankind's activities— the political, the economic, the sociological, the spiritual, and all the rest—only the tremendous social upheaval of war itself has never really been studied with a fundamental and systematic objectivity that would lead the student (and the practitioner) to recognize and better understand a basic pattern of thought, a theory, that did or could influence the conduct of war, influence the basic matter of whether or not a people or a nation might survive.

For so sweeping an assertion as this there must be an almost automatic rebuttal, a putting forward of Clausewitz, of Jomini, of Mahan, or of half a dozen others. It is quite true that such men have been students of warfare, some contemplative, some exploratory, some meticulous, some dogmatic, and some no more than trite and platitudinous. But all of them have in one fashion or another studied and juggled around the detailed specifics or statistics of war. None of them has set himself the task of trying to make a little clearer why wars are managed the way they are. Why does a soldier think like a soldier? Why does a sailor think like a sailor? Why does an airman think like an airman? And then, knowing a little of these problems, the transition to direct application: is this or that strategic thought process an appropriate one to apply to this or that specific situation?

An idea is a very powerful thing, and political ideas or religious ideas or economic ideas have always affected and often controlled the courses of man's destinies. That we understand and accept. So also have strategic ideas influenced or controlled man's destinies, but too few men, including the men who had them, have recognized the controlling strategic concepts and theories hidden behind the glamor or the stench or the vivid, active drama of the war itself.

I cannot help but feel that if we were to understand a little better the paths that are followed by the strategic mind at work, then we might better assess the validity of its product. As a device for historical research this prospect has a fascinating promise—why a war was won or lost, or why it had the result it did—but the real usefulness of the study would, I believe, lie in the possibility of a more searching appraisal of strategies proposed but not yet put to practice.

I intend in this discussion to examine some of the patterns of thought that the military mind does use, and to speculate on some that perhaps it might use.

A better understanding of the military minds and the reasons why they arrive at their opinions, why a general thinks like a soldier and an admiral like a sailor, why an airman stands apart in basic principle from them both, and which of these thought patterns are valid under what circumstances— these are the questions that have not yet been clearly posed, much less been clearly answered.

Professional military men, when they write, usually address themselves to the facts and concrete data they are trained to work with. In doing this they are often admirably precise and clear. On the other hand, the dissection of an idea should more properly be a scholar's job, but the scholars have not done it, and it is difficult to understand why. Of all the great fields into which human energy has been directed, certainly war has caused more trouble than any other. Death and destruction and heartbreak, political upset and economic chaos and social disorder—war involves them all. Yet the scholars have managed with almost serene indifference to ignore the problem of the theories of war and their effect on the conduct of war.*

The literature of war and its strategies is poverty-stricken. Of all the men who have written on the subject of war, I think that only seven have contributed significantly to our better understanding of it and have, by force of idea, influenced the course of it. Chronologically, the ones I have in mind are Machiavelli, Clausewitz, Mahan, Corbett, Douhet, Liddell Hart, and Mao Tse-tung. It may be too soon to include Liddell Hart, but I rather believe that he will grow in stature as time helps to winnow out the contemporary technical comment and leaves the more lasting intellectual contribution. But whether we agree or disagree with any of these men is not relevant. The fact is that they have contributed the influence of idea and in considerable measure affected the course of war and the lives of people. As far as I know only one of them was a trained scholar.† The others forced their way into the thoughts of men by sheer strength of intellect.

---

* There has been a great deal of writing by scholars on military matters in the last two decades, but nearly all of it has been addressed to specific current problems rather than to the conceptual aspects of the use of power. The scholars have been used as problem-solvers. This *ad hoc* approach is simply a continuation of the practice of military men.

† And he was a second-career scholar. Sir Julian Corbett (1854–1922) was educated at Cambridge and called to the bar in the Middle Temple in 1879. He practiced law until 1882, after which he gave his attention to literary affairs. He was a lecturer at the Royal Naval College in 1902, Ford

This book is no pretense at the sorely needed scholarship. It is not intended for that. It does not all hang together with a closely reasoned central theme, and to that extent at least it is undisciplined. One reason for this, and quite probably not the governing reason, is that I have found no really satisfactory comprehensive study of strategy as a whole, though Machiavelli and Liddell Hart have come closer to that than anyone else.

With respect to strategy as a subject of study, its intellectual framework is not clearly outlined, and its vocabulary is almost nonexistent. These two primary tasks are badly in need of doing—the formulation of some kind of an inclusive theoretical model, and the evolution of a vocabulary adequate to its subject. I am afraid they can come to full fruition only when strategy takes its place in the intellectual world along with other social disciplines (or social "sciences" to use the more prevalent but more questionable description). As an area of human activity, warfare and its strategies surely merit that attention.

Before going further in this discussion, three points ought to be made clear.

The first is that we are not talking about battles; we are talking about war. There are plenty of books and there is plenty of good understanding on battles and even on series of battles. But there is precious little study and understanding of the patterns that they form and the plans and concepts that they are a part of. The battles are the technical devices of warfare and its strategies at work in somewhat the sense that

lecturer at Oxford in 1903, and Creighton lecturer at King's College, London, in 1921. Among his books on maritime history are *The Successors of Drake* (1900), *England in the Mediterranean, 1603–1714* (1904), *England in the Seven Years' War* (1907), *The Campaign of Trafalgar* (1910), *Some Principles of Maritime Strategy* (1911), and *Naval Operations* (3 vols., 1921–23).

the manufacture and marketing of automobiles are technical products of an economic system at work. The neglect that I decry is on the study and understanding of strategic systems, potential or applied. It is warfare, not battles, and strategy, not tactics or techniques, that should properly be the social science.

One purpose of this book is to try and demonstrate that it is possible to study warfare, and be both fundamental and practical about it, without dissecting a battle or counting the bullets or tracing the route of the nth division on a large-scale map. What is necessary is that the whole of the thing, all of war, be studied. The fragments of war, the minor parts of strategy, the details of tactics, are quite literally infinite. We know from the hard experiences of the physical and social sciences that if the parts are not ordered in some prior way, are not held up to some broad concept, all we can do is remain the prisoner of raw data. A concept may be wrong or in error, but it should be formulated. So a purpose of this discussion is to be general, to be conceptual, to run initial risks of probing in uncharted areas.

The second point is that there is nothing "secret" about strategy per se. The unwarranted but persistent notion that it is secret may be one reason why it has been so consistently avoided as an intellectual accomplishment. This does not mean that it would be perfectly all right to tell one's opponent what one plans to do in this or that situation; that would be silly. But there is no reason whatever to infer from that that the patterns of thought consciously or more often unconsciously influencing the military mind should be avoided as outside any thinking man's province. Quite the opposite. That kind of an intellectually closed corporation can result only in a sort of intellectual incest and a degeneration into impotent strategic mediocrity. Mutual admiration societies that grow up within little cliques may be fun, but they have not got much vigor. The basic patterns of strategic thought should not be looked on as any kind of a secret. The more people who know about and understand these patterns, the more healthy will be our democracy in its strategic decisions. The Congressman voting on a military appropriation is, in a very real sense indeed, making a fundamental strategic decision, and he does not need very many "secrets" to lead him toward sound decision. The aphorism that war is too important to be left to the generals masks the real situation. None of the really important aspects of strategy is out of the public attention. All that is needed is the combination of interests and skills and methods to study the data.

The third point to be cleared up before going further is this: I do not claim that strategy is or can be a "science" in the sense of the physical sciences. It can and should be an intellectual discipline of the highest order, and the strategist should prepare himself to manage ideas with precision and clarity and imagination in order that his manipulation of physical realities, the tools of war, may rise above the pedestrian plane of mediocrity. Thus, while strategy itself may not be a science, strategic judgment can be scientific to the extent that it is orderly, rational, objective, inclusive, discriminatory, and perceptive. An impressive bag of adjectives, to be sure, but each of them meaningful and at least in some measure necessary to that paragon whom someone would no doubt call the compleat strategist.

CHAPTER TWO

METHODS OF STUDYING STRATEGY

T HERE ARE PROBABLY more kinds of strategy, and more definitions of it, than there are varieties and definitions of economics or politics. It is a loose sort of a word. So in order to avoid confusion and misunderstanding, to provide a focus for this discussion, let me give the definition of strategy that I prefer:

> A plan of action designed in order to achieve some end; a purpose together with a system of measures for its accomplishment.

This definition has two salient features that are relevant to the discussion that follows:

One is that it is a definition not limited to a war situation nor even limited to military application. I believe this condition is necessary for the concept of strategy as an intellectual discipline. In spite of that, I deliberately narrow the field and limit the comments in the pages to follow, with few exceptions, to matters of war or military strategy.

The second salient point of a definition like the one I have chosen is that it enforces a dichotomous thinking—both the purpose and the system of measures to achieve it must be included in the thoughts of the strategist. I think that this is as necessary as the preceding qualification, that of having a concept broader than one limited only to military application.

One can concede readily that it is possible to prepare a plan for doing something with only a vague notion of what the result will be—too many men have done that too often for any of us to believe otherwise—but I do contend that it would be a very difficult job indeed adequately to assess the validity of any strategy without a rather clear appreciation of its purpose.

To illustrate what is meant by this I would suggest that a primary fault in the last war in Europe was that we brilliantly fought and implemented what turned out to be an obscure, contradictory, and finally nonexistent strategic end. Peace, in and of itself, is not necessarily a proper objective, and I do not believe that such reasoning calls for a Machiavellian approach.

But having insisted that both the purpose and the plan for reaching it must be considered in appraising a strategy, I should like to double back and say that the appraisal is a two-part process. Analysis must be applied to both parts, and one can see many situations in which the analyses of the two would be quite different.

This division of strategy into two major segments permits us to digress for a moment and to look at each of them separately, allowing us to settle one element of confusion at the very start. This has to do with the frequently encountered classification of "good" and "bad" strategies in a moral sense. It should be recognized at the outset of this discussion that a strategy has no moral quality of its own. It is inherently neither good nor evil; it is always normative or concerned with values. The morality of a strategy can only be measured in terms of the cultural value judgments of the critics. Brilliant measures may be applied for "evil" ends; or dull, unimaginative, or completely inadequate plans may be adopted in hopes of reaching the most praiseworthy goals.

The comparative morality of both the purpose and the system of measures adopted to form a strategy does, however, have a considerable effect on the validity of the entire strategy for at least two reasons. First, if the purpose of the strategy turns out to be of dubious moral quality in the eyes of the strategist, it may to that extent be self-defeating. And second, the morality of the strategist, the executors, or the presumed benefactors, imposes definite limits on both the purposes and the systems of measures that may be considered for adoption. These self-imposed limitations of moral judgments (under whatever standards) operate quite effectively to restrict the choices open to strategists to a sometimes rather narrow portion of the entire spectrum of possibilities. Recognition of this type of self-imposed limitation may help explain, for instance, some of the otherwise inscrutable moves of the communists in their application or withholding of political and other types of force in the last forty years. It is certainly an understandable basis for some of the trepidation with which a good many men assay the prospect of nuclear weapons. Although strategy itself may be as neutral as physics or physiology, the moral climates in which it operates may sharply limit the range of acceptable strategies in any particular situation.*

So now, with a working description to supply a point of departure, and the incidental stumbling block of strategic morality set more or less in place, we find ourselves faced with the major business at hand. How does one bite into the problem of studying strategy in the abstract? Where does one start? How does one dissect war to study its strategy and the intellectual platforms on which it is built? And then how might one build a better strategy when the time comes?

There are several paths that have been followed, and we should look at some of them to decide where we stand.

The classical method is that of the poet and the historian. Each of them tells us a tale, in his own fashion, of the drama and the data of war. One of them gives us the feel and the

---

* A somewhat different approach to the problem of the moral factors in strategy may be found in Henry E. Eccles' *Military Concepts and Philosophy* (Rutgers, 1965), pp. 32–34.

other the facts of war. And both of them are a needed prelude for the study of war. But the analyst must go further than either, and perhaps in a different direction.

In looking about in the fields of strategic studies we would early find a rather frequently used attitudinal description of war-phases or strategy-phases for which the military terms today (we do have a vocabulary here) are "defensive," sometimes gradations such as "defensive-offensive," and "offensive." There are lesser subdivisions for which the terminology—such as "delaying," "holding," "probing," and the like—is clearly meaningful, though as it becomes more precise it becomes at the same time more technical and restrictive, and less useful to our newly charted needs.

There has been a good deal written on war and strategy in this vein. Some of it is very good and correspondingly useful. Clausewitz managed to discuss war, using among others this mode of entry into the subject, with a sophistication that has so far been unexcelled. In this ability, though, he is virtually alone. Others have used a variation of this technique for a sort of reportorial analysis and used it with considerable skill though in a quite different fashion. The war reports of the United States chiefs of services during and after World War II are succinct masterpieces that employ this war-phase breakdown to achieve an effective operational chronology. So effective, indeed, that it seems to have profoundly influenced the succeeding generation in each of their professions.

It does not seem, however, that this method of opening up the problem offers a great deal of hope either for penetrating analysis or for practical application in the strategic planning process. Clausewitz, in those parts of his writings in which he used this kind of analysis, is not sufficiently inclusive nor is he sufficiently fundamental in that he does not reach to the heart of the problem—the strategic patterns of thought from which grow the actions of war itself. He does, to be sure, go into the conduct of campaigns, and he does make incisive comment

17

on such matters as the psychological effects of offense and defense; but these, while perhaps as valid today as they were then, are peripheral to the central core of our inquiry. In general, most of his observations based on this foundation of reasoning do not have much of a substantive transfer value from his time to ours.

With respect to the apparent tendency today to use this classification as a strategic planning technique, I think there is a fatal defect. The war reports by the service chiefs were based on historic fact, and their "defense" or "offense" classifications for descriptive purposes served as a convenient and usable device to present the war and its strategies in an intelligible, as well as emotionally acceptable, context.

There are two objections to this. One is that the idea of "offense" for the sake of the emotionally desirable idea of attacking is without clear purpose, and at least to that extent is a formless concept. Second, the very fact that they were histories is a critical weakness when this method is adapted to planning. The method is, necessarily, post hoc—it comes after the event, it is retrospect. There must be some facts before there can be this kind of classification, and if the facts have not yet come to pass they must be assumed. This or that situation must be assumed before there can be any thinking ahead on strategy based on attitudinal classifications, and thus the "defense-offense" military mind finds itself deep in the treacherous business of forecasting the events of a hypothetical war whether aware of it or not. Reserving until later more detailed comment on this sticky question of assumptions, I believe that these two objections to this particular method of attack on the problem are ample reason to reject it in its present form as an unpromising lead to better analysis of strategic patterns of thought.

Another method of discussing warfare in the abstract is by isolation of certain "Principles of War." This kind of analytic device, in the past as well as today, is a method often favored by military men themselves as well as by writers when they turn to general discussion of the military profession.

There are anywhere from eight or ten to a dozen and a half of these "principles," depending on whose listing one happens to have at hand. Most lists contain such components as the "principle of the objective," the "principle of the offensive," the "principle of concentration," the "principle of security," and so on.

As men become wiser these listings are improved upon. There is sometimes a remarkable quality of timeliness in these essences of wisdom, such as one that came to light a few years back. For a couple of generations at least, there had been unquestioned acceptance among the advocates that the "principle of cooperation" was a fundamental quality of success in warfare. Quite probably it was. But during the rough and bitter arguments over the first legislation creating a Department of Defense, one service restudied this matter and quietly dropped the "principle of cooperation" from its official publications. It was replaced by the "principle of unity of command."

The principles are clear and simple lasting truths. There can be no doubt about them. The Reds concentrated and beat the Whites in '72; the Blacks concentrated and beat the Greens in '86; ergo, concentration per se is an essential ingredient of victory. Thus we arrive at the distilled wisdom of the centuries: the "principle of concentration" is an immutable truth. This is the presentation of the "principles" that one normally encounters. This is also logical nonsense.

The joker is displayed in the little explanation that somehow creeps into all the better dissertations and lectures on this subject, a qualification to the effect that the wise commander must know when and how to apply the principles and also when and how to violate them. No one that I know of has ever discussed the very practical matter of how the principles are used to generate a strategy.

I think that what the principles really are is an attempt to rationalize and categorize common sense. I am not at all sure whether it is either necessary or possible to teach common sense; but I am very sure indeed that the subject of strategic analysis and understanding is not to be coped with by any such elemental and facile tabulations as these. At the risk of treading on the toes of sincere and able men, I suggest that worship of any such patter as the "principles of war" is an unaware substitution of slogan for thought, probably brought about by the intellectual formlessness that must inevitably exist when there is no orderly and disciplined pattern of fundamental theory from which one consciously or unconsciously takes departure. What I am trying to describe here is the existence of a sort of amiable and well-intentioned intellectual anarchy.

A considerably more sophisticated approach to strategic studies, in fairly wide use in this country and in Great Britain today, is the effort better to prepare prospective strategists for their work by a deliberate broadening of their horizons in study of social matters that have an inevitably close relationship to military action. It includes studies in such fields as political factors impinging on military strategy, economic factors, social factors, and so on. This kind of study cannot help but improve the quality of the strategies these men may devise. But the process of enlarging the military strategist's appreciation of the environment in which he functions, and of enforcing in his mind an integration of the social divisions of strategy, does not bear directly on the subject of strategic patterns of thought and is not, of itself, an intellectual tool for better analysis of these patterns.

In addition to those already mentioned, there may well be a dozen other ways to slice into the problem, but so far I have uncovered only two, both of which are presented in the pages that follow. One is a type of analysis by operational pattern, and the other is analysis on a conceptual or theoretical foundation. Neither is yet commonly recognized, and I believe both hold some promise. To some extent they overlap, though the second (the theoretical) is the more embracing and more fundamental and thus should be the more productive field for study.

In considering these two, one now and one later on, it should be recognized that they are not patterns of thought that are now in common use for analytical purposes. They are patterns that might be developed and might profitably be used, both by the military mind in actual work and by the armchair strategist in study and in historical analysis.

CHAPTER THREE

CUMULATIVE AND SEQUENTIAL STRATEGIES

A FEW YEARS AGO, in an article in the U.S. Naval Institute *Proceedings,** I suggested a method of analysis in terms of two hitherto unrecognized general operational patterns of strategies. It landed with no splash at the time and has lain on the deck ever since. I still think it holds some promise, so I will restate it briefly.

In taking up these two operationally different kinds of strategies, we must use descriptive adjectives not conventionally used in strategic conversations (the vocabulary problem mentioned earlier is evident here). The classifications will be "sequential" and "cumulative" strategies. This type of analysis was suggested by the late Dr. Herbert Rosinski in conversations in the spring of 1951. He used the terms "directive" and "cumulative," and my development of his basic idea may or may not be the same as his. It is a pity that he did not find time to address himself more fully to this intriguing subject.

Normally we consider a war as a series of discrete steps or actions, with each one of this series of actions growing naturally out of, and dependent on, the one that preceded it. The total pattern of all the discrete or separate actions makes up,

---

* U.S. Naval Institute *Proceedings,* Vol. 78, No. 4 (April, 1952), pp. 360–61. [Reprinted as Appendix A to this edition.—Ed.]

serially, the entire sequence of the war. If at any stage of the war one of these actions had happened differently, then the remainder of the sequence would have had a different pattern. The sequence would have been interrupted and altered.

The two great drives across the Pacific in World War II— MacArthur's campaign in the Southwest Pacific and the Central Pacific drive from Hawaii to the coast of China—can be analyzed as sequential strategies. So, too, can we analyze the drive to Germany from the Normandy landings or the German drive into Russia. Each of these was composed of a series of discrete steps, and each step could be clearly seen by the strategist ahead of time, could be clearly appraised in terms of its expected result; and the actual result in turn would lead to the next step, the next position to be taken, or the next action to be planned. That is what is meant by reference to a sequential strategy.

But there is another way to prosecute a war. There is a type of warfare in which the entire pattern is made up of a collection of lesser actions, but these lesser or individual actions are not sequentially interdependent. Each individual one is no more than a single statistic, an isolated plus or minus, in arriving at the final result.

Psychological warfare might be such a matter, for instance, or economic warfare. No one action is completely dependent on the one that preceded it. The thing that counts is the cumulative effect. For a military example of this cumulative strategy we may look to the submarine campaigns in the Atlantic or in the Pacific in World War II.

The tonnage war waged by the American submarines in the Pacific was quite unlike the serial, the sequential, type of strategy. In a tonnage war it is not possible to forecast, with any degree of accuracy, the result of any specific action.

Any such war as these tonnage wars is an accumulation of more or less random individual victories. Any single submarine action is only one independent element in the cumulative effect of the total campaign.

So, in the Pacific from 1941 to 1945, we seem to have conducted two separate wars against Japan. We conducted the sequential strategy campaigns, our drives across the Pacific to the coast of Asia and up to the shores of the Empire. And apparently quite apart from them we conducted a cumulative strategy aimed primarily at Japan's economy. These two went along together in time but were essentially independent in the day-to-day activity.

We were able, with some degree of accuracy, to predict in advance the outcome of the sequential strategy. We were not able, or at least we seem not to have taken full advantage of whatever ability we had, to predict the compounding effect of the cumulative strategy as it operated concurrently with and was enhanced by the sequential strategy. Sometime in 1944 we brought Japan, in large measure by the ever-increasing pressure of this cumulative strategy, to a condition in which she had only two alternatives: to give in, or to approach national suicide. We are not, even today, able to tell precisely when that took place. But it did take place. Japan started the war with about six million tons of shipping. During the early years of the war she acquired almost four million more. But by late 1944 nearly nine of this total of ten million tons had been destroyed. Japan had long since passed her point of no return. But we seemed not to know it, and possibly the Japanese did not know it.

The point to be made is this: there are actually two very different kinds of strategies that may be used in war. One is the sequential, the series of visible, discrete steps, each dependent on the one that preceded it. The other is the cumulative, the less perceptible minute accumulation of little items piling one on top of the other until at some unknown point the mass of accumulated actions may be large enough to be critical. They are not incompatible strategies, they are not mutually exclusive. Quite the opposite. In practice they are usually interdependent in their strategic result.

The sequential strategies all of us probably understand; the cumulative possibly we do not. The latter, the cumulative, has long been a characteristic of war at sea and may be a characteristic of air warfare. But there has been no conscious analytical differentiation of this cumulative warfare from the sequential in any of the major writings on strategy; and there is no major instance in which a cumulative strategy, operating by itself, has been successful. The French, for instance, were long addicted to their *guerre de course* at sea, but they never had it pay off in decisive victory by itself. The Germans have twice concentrated all their maritime effort on a cumulative strategy and have twice seen it fail. It would be interesting to analyze both the German air effort against Great Britain and the Allied air effort against Germany on this basis.

But when these cumulative strategies have been used in conjunction with a sequential strategy, directed at a critical point within the enemy structure, there are many instances in which the strength of the cumulative strategy has meant the difference between success or failure of the sequential. History abounds with examples in which a comparatively weak sequential strategy was enabled to reach victory by virtue of the strength of the cumulative strategy behind it. The Yorktown Campaign, the Peninsula Campaign in Portugal, or our own War between the States are three that come to mind. The First World War is another example. In the Second World War, both in Europe and in the Pacific, we seem not to have fully appreciated the strengths of our cumulative strategies operating as they did in support of the sequential thrusts to the critical goals.

Recognition of these two basically different kinds of strategies may open up a new area for the exercise of strategic skills. Our strategic success in the future may be measured in great part by the skill with which we are able to balance our sequential and cumulative efforts toward the most effective and least costly attainment of our goals. If we could judge the progress and the effect of our cumulative strategy, not only would we control an important element of our strategy that up to now we have been forced to leave largely to chance, but we might more effectively shape the conditions existing when the war is over.

So two specific suggestions: we should recognize the existence and power of these cumulative strategies and integrate them more carefully into our basic strategic thinking; and we should study them more closely than we have in order that we might be able to determine whether or not they profitably could be critical—and if they could, then identify the points in their development at which they do become critical determinants in the progress of war. When we do that we will be able to use them more efficiently and economically than we have in the past.

These illustrations are derived primarily from maritime warfare, and from submarine warfare in particular. It is suggested, however, if they have application in the situation today when so much of our attention is necessarily focused in the air, that a major utility is likely to be found in their application not only to submarine but to aerial warfare; and in this sense we should include both aircraft and missiles. One can sense a very real possibility that this concept of sequential and cumulative strategies operating in coordination may help us form more valid judgments of the interrelationship between ground and air, ground and sea, and sea and air forces. If, as prior experience seems to indicate, a cumulative strategy is not of itself reliably decisive, then study may be in order to see just when and how a sequential strategy may be most efficiently brought to bear to reinforce and take advantage of it.

The direct application to today's problem might well be in determination of the most efficient method of combining cumulative maritime and air strategies with sequential maritime and continental strategies.

In suggesting this technique as an aid in forming strategic concepts, I do so with two reservations. First, this concept of two different kinds of operational patterns is not, in itself, an adequate basis for the concept of warfare in its entirety. Rather than that, it may be a conceptual device that can be used within the outlines of one or more theories of warfare or war strategy that will be taken up shortly.

And second, it is not implied that this operational-pattern concept can be systematized to the extent that it is susceptible to anything so concrete as rigid mathematical tabulations.*

If there is use to be found in this, it is as an intellectual avenue of approach, a reference concept within the bounds of which one might weigh this possible outcome against that one. Nothing more, I fear, than that.

---

* [The author has since revised his thoughts on cumulative strategies. See page 101 in the postscript.—Ed.]

CHAPTER FOUR

THE CASE FOR THEORY IN STRATEGY

A GOOD DEAL of the discussion up to this point has been rather sharply critical of the approaches to the study of warfare that have been in general favor, or at least in general practice, for a good many years.

I have lamented the fact that there has been too little disciplined effort made to study warfare in its totality—and this has no connection with "total war"—and that there has been little or no recognition that the study of warfare merits a place in the intellectual world as a matter worthy of more than technical study.

This criticism is applicable to two groups of people: First, to the scholars who have not seen the need for their assistance—and if they bristle at this, let them compare how many doctoral theses have been written on warfare and how many on such weighty matters as the place of county governments in highway building programs, or the function of the branch bank in the credit system of the 1920s. And second, to my own profession in all its branches for not putting more effort on the fundamental problem of the conceptual foundation of its profession.

Of the two, the second may be the less important criticism because, as practitioners, the military profession has so far produced more than enough brilliant men to successfully direct the military strength of their country when it has been called upon to do so.

The fact of the matter is that at least three of the specific theories of warfare that I will discuss are quite reasonably understood by the men who practice them. The fault one might find is that, by and large, they do not recognize that they are following, and are indeed bound by, definite theories. The handicaps of this intuitive, as opposed to conscious and analytic, understanding are at least two in number.

In not having a conscious and analytic appreciation of their own patterns of thought, the military minds in too many cases are restricted to the limits of their intuitive thoughts that, after a lifetime of largely technical training, are perhaps somewhat narrower than they might be. A more general theoretical appreciation should give a greater breadth to the vision of the strategist. The recognized possibilities for action would increase in number.

Then, too, this limitation to intuitive appreciation of one's own theory of strategy almost automatically inhibits adequate appreciation of any others. This has the very real effect of at least partially blocking communication between the practitioners of different theories. One man thinks like a soldier, the next like a sailor, and so on. The remarkable thing is not that there is so much disagreement in the Pentagon but that there is so much agreement. It is a tribute to the character of the men in the services that, with so little in the way of organized and disciplined conceptual tools to use in their analyses, they have, by a unique application of will power and what might be called brute-force application of intelligence, come so far toward appreciation of each other's positions and toward the correlation of their common efforts.

It is my firm belief that if there were general recognition that there are in actual operation today at least four—and possibly more—valid and practical theories of strategy, there

29

would be a far better chance of an intensive, inclusive, and incisive study of the prospects before any strategy was finally adopted. There would then be opportunity for the strategist to survey the situation confronting him, to judge whether this concept or that one or what combination of them would be most appropriate, and then to tailor his plans accordingly, having had the widest possible field for his intellect to operate in.

If the sailor, for instance, were more analytically—rather than only technically and intuitively—familiar with the airman's pattern of thought, he would be able, in discussions with airmen, to think more like an airman; and the shared areas of common understanding would be greater. And the same for the soldier or the airman in reverse—and if I suggest that this might be more markedly so in the second case, perhaps that is because I am a sailor displaying my bias to prove my point.

In summation, a more thorough recognition and appreciation of the several patterns of thoughts that make up our military minds would probably produce better strategies.

It is appropriate here to inject a reminder that all the military minds, the strategists, in this country are not in uniform. A very important number of them have spent all of their lives—except perhaps for war service—as civilians, and only a small part of those lifetimes has been spent in study of strategic problems.

But again a caution: I do not mean that admirals and generals and majors and ensigns, or Congressmen or journalists or civil officials of government, should all take a year's leave of absence and turn themselves into strategic theorists. The continuing evolution and refinement of the theories should be a task for the scholars, not for the practicing military men. I do believe, however, that the men who control or influence strategy should recognize that the theories do exist, should appreciate that the theories do in fact influence the strategic mind at work whether those minds realize it or not, and should understand the general conceptual framework within which they and their colleagues actually practice their professions.

One thing more before we get on. A theory in any such slippery field as that of strategy is not itself something real and tangible; it is not something that actually has concrete existence. A theory is simply an idea designed to account for actuality or to account for what the theorist thinks will come to pass as actuality. It is orderly rationalization of real or presumed patterns of events. A basic measure of validity of any theory is how closely the postulates of the theory coincide with reality in any actual situation. If any military theory has any proven validity, it is because some practicing military man has actually given it that validity in a real situation. The theory serves a useful purpose to the extent that it can collect and organize the experiences and ideas of other men, sort out which of them may have a valid transfer value to a new and different situation, and help the practitioner to enlarge his vision in an orderly, manageable and useful fashion—and then apply it to the reality with which he is faced.

CHAPTER FIVE

THE EXISTING
THEORIES

THERE ARE NOW in existence three generally recognized major theories of war strategy and one newly emergent. Nearly all practicing strategists, in uniform or otherwise, are either conscious or unaware devotees of one or another of them. They will be identified in this discussion as the continental, the maritime, and the air theories, and the Mao theory of the "wars of national liberation."

The histories and evolution and construction of these four are not similar, and in many respects it is difficult to compare them and weigh them off one against another.

The continental theory is the loosest of the four insofar as its structure and clarity are concerned. It consists in large part of one central theme plus a great deal of experience and common sense, leavened by bits and pieces of doctrine and lore, held together by some generally unrecognized assumptions, and limited by the writings of those few men who have addressed themselves to the problem of the strategic direction of armies.

The maritime theory as such is only a few decades in print, although its practice has several hundred years of evolution behind it. It reached its classic apex in Britain's waging of the Napoleonic Wars, lay quiescent for a century and a half, and then reached a new peak of practical perfection in the Second World War.

The air theory, now so prominent in the minds of all the world, is unique in that it was born as an idea rather than developed from experience. It has never been adequately put to practice. Indeed, there are many who have held that it would never be worked out in practice as it has been postulated in theory, although I, for one, believe it has today a high degree of potential validity within the bounds of its limiting assumptions.

The Mao theory of political warfare is by far the most sophisticated of the current theories of war. It, more clearly than any other, states its purpose and sets forth the systems of measures for its accomplishment. That its purpose is political, and that its systems of measures include political, social, and economic as well as military measures is an indication of both the scope and the realism of the theory in practice. This theory, more than any other, is attuned to the prevailing fact of the world-wide social revolution of this century. Indeed, an appreciable portion of this revolution is the product of the Mao theory in action.

I. THE MARITIME THEORY

Since the maritime theory has both a long record of practice and a fairly clear pattern of theory, it would perhaps be simplest to discuss it first.*

It consists, briefly, of two major parts: the establishment of control of the sea, and the exploitation of the control of the sea toward establishment of control on the land.

The establishment of control of the sea was first described in a clear and structurally complete form by Corbett, barely

---

* Some of the ideas on this subject appeared in different form in an article of mine in the U.S. Naval Institute *Proceedings,* Vol. 83, No. 8 (August, 1957), pp. 811–17. [Reprinted as Appendix B to this edition.—Ed.]

33

more than a generation ago. Mahan sensed it before Corbett and wrote all around and about it, but never did quite put his finger on it. He did not summarize his thoughts in clear, inclusive general terms, nor did he succinctly set forth a model strategy for maritime warfare. What Mahan became famous for, and quite properly so, was his recognition of the role of sea power as a basis for national policy. Prior to the middle of the twentieth century no one had set forth in writing the second half of the maritime theory of warfare, the exploitation of control at sea toward the establishment of control on the land.

This is not to say that the complete pattern was not well understood, if not articulately expressed, at least two hundred years ago—merely that it had never, until recently, been described in general or theoretical terms and set down on paper for analytic discussion.

The establishment of control of the sea means, in its ideal form, complete knowledge and complete control of everything that moves by sea. This ideal was approached but never reached in the older wars, and only in the latter stages of World War II in late 1944 and 1945 was it attained in an essentially absolute sense. A governing degree of control rather than an absolute control is probably all that need be striven for in most practical situations.

The matters of limited control, local control, or transient control of the sea are all relevant to a detailed inquiry but are not necessary for a general discussion of this nature.

Prior to the Second World War, the second or exploitation phase of the maritime theory of strategy was a diffuse and indirect process. The pressure of exploitation was exerted largely through economic avenues with the resultant political and social by-products reinforcing the economic pressure. The blockade in all its forms and ramifications was a principal tool of exploitation of maritime strength. Of intermittent importance as a means of maritime exploitation was the injection and support of armies in a sensitive land area, a process that was possible only to the power exercising control at sea.

Wellington in the Peninsula Campaign in Portugal and Spain and Washington at Yorktown would have faced impossible situations had their colleagues on the sea not done their work beforehand. Napoleon looking across the Channel was faced by a problem so vast that he never understood it in all its magnitude. He simply turned away. Perhaps one of his spies had relayed to him the classic comment ascribed to the Earl of St. Vincent at a meeting of the war council discussing the prospect of French invasion of the British Isles. The First Sea Lord is reported to have said, "I do not say the Frenchman will not come, I only say he will not come by sea."

Except for a few isolated instances of gallant men storming ramparts—Wolfe at Quebec was one—the very idea of forcible injection of troops directly from the sea into combat ashore was nearly impossible until the last few decades. The technical requirements, the tools, for the protection and support and intercommunication and management of an amphibious assault were not available until some time after the First World War.

It was only during the Second World War that men had at hand the means they needed for the direct intrusion of their soldiery from the sea into combat ashore. The boats, the vehicles, the armor, the guns, the radios, and their correlation and management techniques needed for amphibious assault against determined resistance only became available in time for the Second World War. This means that only toward the middle of this present century do we see the possibility of complete military accomplishment of the basic pattern of maritime strategy, a pattern that up to that time had been precise and clear-cut in its first phase but devious and subtle in the slow but effective workings of its second, workings that in large measure were economic and political rather than military.

An even more recent technological extension of the second phase of the maritime concept—the exploitation of control at sea toward establishment of control on the land—is the submarine-launched Polaris missile. To be effective, these missile-launching submarines must be relatively secure from preemptive suppression before their missiles are launched. This pre-launch security comes from a degree of control of the sea, and it paves the way for the second phase, the extension of power from the sea onto the land. It should be noted that the extension of control onto the land in this case is hinged upon the destructive power of the missile, which is a highly specialized but by no means unusual method of exercising control. More readily taken up in connection with the air theory, this relation of destruction to control will be enlarged upon after the air concept has been introduced.

II. THE AIR THEORY

As indicated earlier, the air theory is unique in the sense that it exists primarily as theory rather than as a system of tested experiments that have grown gradually into a meaningful pattern over the years.

There is considerable argument as to whether modern air forces are actually based on Douhet's theory.* Many of to-

---

* In *The Military Intellectuals in Britain, 1918–1939* (Rutgers University Press, 1966), Robin Higham devotes an appendix to "The Place of Douhet." On page 258 he says, ". . . it seems quite clear that Douhet had no influence in the forming of British airpower theory." Certainly Trenchard in Great Britain and Mitchell and, later, LeMay in the United States were all-powerful exponents of the air theory. I cite Douhet in this book because he was the one who most clearly put his ideas in print, and I do believe he had a great deal of influence in the United States.

day's practitioners vaguely resent an imputation to this effect, but most of those who have studied the problem in any depth do agree that the Douhet postulations are a valid point of departure for modern air warfare theories. General H. H. Arnold, in his *Global Mission*, recognized the Douhet theory as an intellectual basis and referred to "the United States' modifications of the Douhet theories, which we had been teaching as an abstract science at the Air Corps Tactical School for several years" (in the nineteen thirties).

So, in spite of some disagreement as to current relevance, Douhet will be used here as the best basic source of the air theory concepts.

A little before the First World War Giulio Douhet became convinced that the coming of the airplane meant a radical revolution in warfare. In a series of discussions in the Italian professional journals he set forth his beliefs and then expanded and reissued them in book form in 1921 and 1927. Other men in other countries, in part independently and in part influenced by Douhet, arrived at the same general thesis as the Italian pioneer.

Douhet's basic beliefs, as he outlined them in *The Command of the Air,** are as follows:

> The form of any war . . . depends on the technical means of war available. [p. 6]
> . . . Two new weapons, the air arm and poison gas . . . will completely upset all forms of war so far known . . . [p. 6]
> Air power makes it possible not only to make bombing raids over any sector of the enemy's territory, but also to ravage his whole country by chemical and bacteriological warfare. [pp. 6–7]
> There is no doubt now that half of the destruction wrought by the war [World War I] would have been enough if it had been accomplished in three months instead of four years. A

* Originally published in 1921 and 1927; translated by Dino Ferrari and published in English by Coward-McCann, New York, in 1942.

quarter of it would have been sufficient if it had been wrought in eight days. [p. 14]

. . . there is no practical way to prevent the enemy from attacking us with his air force except to destroy his air power before he has a chance to strike at us. [p. 18]

This is the logical and rational concept . . . to prevent the enemy from flying or from carrying out any aerial action at all. [p. 19]

In general, aerial offensives will be directed against such targets as peacetime industrial and commercial establishments; important buildings, private and public; transportation arteries and centers; and certain designated areas of civilian population as well . . . three kinds of bombs are needed. . . . The explosives will demolish the target, the incendiaries set fire to it, and the poison-gas bombs prevent fire fighters from extinguishing the fires. [p. 20]

To have command of the air means to be in a position to prevent the enemy from flying while retaining the ability to fly oneself. [p. 24]

A nation which has command of the air is in a position to . . . put a halt to the enemy's auxiliary actions [elsewhere described as air components of ground and naval forces] in support of his land and sea operations, thus leaving him powerless to do much of anything. [p. 25]

To conquer the command of the air means victory; to be beaten in the air means defeat and acceptance of whatever terms the enemy may be pleased to impose . . . which . . . is an axiom. [p. 28]

From this axiom we come immediately to this first corollary: *In order to assure an adequate national defense, it is necessary—and sufficient—to be in a position in case of war to conquer the command of the air.* And from that we arrive at this second corollary: *All that a nation does to assure her own defense should have as its aim procuring for herself those means which, in case of war, are most effective for the conquest of command of the air.* [p. 28]

Any diversion from this primary purpose is an error.[p. 28]

... ask only that we give the air arm the importance it deserves ... *a progressive decrease of land and sea forces, accompanied by a corresponding increase of aerial forces until they are strong enough to conquer the command of the air.* [p. 30]

This new character of war ... will ... make for swift, crushing decisions ... [p. 30]

We must therefore resign ourselves to the offensives the enemy inflicts upon us, while striving to put all our resources to work to inflict even heavier ones upon him. [p. 55]

An Independent Air Force must therefore be completely free of any preoccupation with the actions of the enemy force. [p. 59]

... the only aerial organization whose existence is fully justified is the Independent Air Force. [p. 95]

Effort has been made here to avoid using quotations that are distorted when lifted out of context, and the obviously local references with which Douhet's writings abound have been purposely omitted. These extracts are intended to present an honest crosscut of a very important pattern of thought.

If one looks at Douhet as a cue to a pattern of thought, then it becomes quite easy to understand the thread of argument in the decade following World War II by some of the proponents of air power and the independent and dominant air force. The roster of proponents was a large and impressive one and contained the names of men who were then and are now among the most respected in the nation.

Review for a moment some of the aviation themes of the decade following World War II:

—the independence of military aviation, particularly bomber aviation, both during World War II and in the organizational autonomy of heavy bombers since that time,

—the "interdiction" concept of the "isolation of the battle-

39

field," which generated considerable discussion between airmen and soldiers as to the relative importance of interdiction
and direct air support at the scene of battle (both are now
generally recognized as necessary and valid requirements),

—the command relationship matters between soldiers and
aviators in which the aviator must be as close to autonomy as
possible,

—the ready extension of the Douhet thesis into what a decade ago was described as "preventive war." This was a very
touchy subject indeed, and some of the less thoughtful speak-
ers on this subject took a rather extreme position on this
some years ago. The full implications seem now well understood, and there has been little or no public comment in this
vein in recent years.

—the budgetary emphasis in the fifties on strategic bombing as contrasted, for instance, with close support of troops
and similar tasks not included as central in the Douhet theory.

—the quick war, all over in ten or thirty or ninety days.

It should be clearly stated here that this is not an accurate
picture of the subject matter set forth either today or as early
as the middle 1950s in *United States Air Force Basic Doctrine* (dated April 1955). No attempt is made here to present
"official" positions, but rather to illustrate that attitudes and
actions of a very important intellectual segment have had a
clearly reasoned theoretical basis.

The apparent validity of the Douhet theory is interesting to
trace. Prior to World War II it existed only in idea. During
that war it was put, at least in part, to practical test. The results can be (and have been) argued in almost any way that
one might choose—either that it was proven, that it was dis-
proven, or that opportunity was never granted to put the theory adequately to practice.

At any rate, Douhet's theory in its complete form was, by
June of 1945, seriously questioned by a good many critics un-

til shortly after that date the appearance of the first atomic bomb radically altered this aspect of warfare.

Nuclear weapons, more than anything except flight itself, have served to enhance the potential validity of Douhet's ideas. Where Douhet spoke of poison gas, we can read nuclear weapons; and if we accept the basic assumption that destruction is equivalent to control, then a high degree of potential validity attaches to the thesis.

There are three problems associated with the air theory today.

One is the question of whether nuclear weapons will in fact be used. Answers to this are far beyond military determination; the military problem is to be prepared for both contingencies, use and nonuse.

A second problem is the effect of the exploding space technology. Are air theories extensible into aerospace theories? Many able men are wrestling today with this problem, and just what the modified theory or the successor theory will be is yet unclear. Whatever it is, it will have to be hinged in some way to a correlation between destruction and control.

The third problem, not yet adequately answered, can be set forth quite briefly. What kind of control is desired, and under what circumstances will destruction or the threat of destruction bring about the desired measure of control? Judgments of this kind are among the most difficult and speculative of all the problems of strategy.

III. THE CONTINENTAL THEORY

These, then, are the bases of the sailor's and the airman's conceptions of strategy-in-action. What of the soldiers?

First, the connotation of the word "strategy" is not the same to the soldier as to the sailor or airman. The reason for this is elusive but very real. It has to do with the environment in which the conception is set.

41

Where the sailor or airman think in terms of an entire world, the soldier at work thinks in terms of theaters, in terms of campaigns, or in terms of battles. And the three concepts are not too markedly different from each other.

This state of mind in which the soldier derives his conception of the strategic scene is brought about primarily by the matter of geography. Prominent and direct in its effect is the fundamental fact of terrain. "Terrain" as a word does not have deep meaning to the nonsoldier, but to the soldier it is everything. It is the fixed field within which he operates. It is the limitation within which he must function. It is the opponent that he must always face no matter who may be his enemy. It is the fact of terrain that establishes the field within which the soldier's professional intellect must generate its plans.

Where the sailor and the airman are almost forced, by the nature of the sea and the air, to think in terms of a total world or, at the least, to look outside the physical limits of their immediate concerns, the soldier is almost literally hemmed in by his terrain.

From this fact of terrain as a limited element has come the concept of "theater" in the soldier's strategy, a terrain division somehow arbitrary to the sailor or the airman but sound and logical if we move into the soldier's headquarters. The idea of theater in the soldier's conception of matters strategic is both a symptom of his physical restrictions and a direct result of it. Consider Napoleon's comment to the effect that natural boundaries are mountains and deserts and rivers—this from the man who stood utterly and permanently thwarted on the shores of the English Channel.

Terrain. The point of departure for the soldier's conception of warfare. Do not derogate it. The soldier in his environment is perfectly right. It will always be there, and it is the only place that humans can live. But recognize at the same time that, while to the soldier it is fundamental, to the sailor or to the airman it need be only the goal at which one must arrive. It need not also be the same terrain in which one starts.

A second factor of primary influence in the soldier's strategic pattern of thought, related closely to the status of terrain, is the nature of the soldier's combat—and thus the nature of his conception of strategy.

The sailor and the airman encounter war as a separated series of encounters. After each encounter the two sides separate. They haul off, they regroup, they jockey again for position, and to a considerable extent each combatant retains to himself the decision as to whether and where and when to fight again. In most situations, the sailor and the airman fight with their opponents only when, for one reason or another, it is mutually agreeable. Mahan and perhaps others before him have found it convenient to differentiate tactical and strategic matters by the simple fact of contact. When opposing forces are in contact, the plans and operations are "tactical." Everything outside contact is "strategic."

Not so the soldier. His conception of the separation of strategy and tactics, and thus his concept of the scope of strategy, is on an entirely different footing. The "contact" thumb rule has no validity for him. The soldier makes contact when the war starts, and he makes every effort to maintain contact until the war is over. The soldier who has lost contact with his enemy is in a bad way. To the soldier the shading between a tactic and a strategy is a fuzzy and not too important one.

There is more truth than jest in the statement that, to any soldier, what he does is tactical and what his next senior does is strategic. This is generally expressive from the private all the way up to the theater commander. There seems fairly unchallenged agreement among soldiers that the senior officer of the Army in a multitheater war has a strategic problem. But below him the problems rapidly become tactical, not strategic, with the theater commander (the influence of terrain) being the juncture at which strategic directives received metamorphose into tactical orders issued.

From these two elements—the fact of terrain and its unquestioned importance as the scene of human activity, and the fact that contact is essential and continuous in land warfare—from these two influences is derived the third governing factor in the soldier's strategic pattern of thought. It can best be expressed by direct quotation from a mid-1950 version of the Field Service Regulations: "The ultimate objective of all military operations is the destruction of the enemy's armed forces and his will to fight."* This sums up the gist of the soldier's theoretical concept of war strategy in one succinct sentence. It is axiomatic to the Clausewitz theorist that the aim of war is defeat of the enemy's armed forces. The theme runs all through Clausewitz and all through his successors and his interpreters. After that is done, after the enemy army is met and defeated, then all the other needed things will fall into place. General Eisenhower spoke for the soldier in his *Crusade in Europe*. Referring to one of Mr. Churchill's political interests, he said: "For this concern I had great sympathy, but as a soldier I was particularly careful to exclude such considerations from my own recommendations." (p. 194)

In no way is any judgment implied that this was good or bad. It is cited to shed light on the soldier's concept of warfare. It is focused directly on the enemy army, and it is just as direct and clear-cut as the soldier can make it.

The classical soldier's beliefs and behavior patterns are all summarized in the central theme of Clausewitz, who tells us that his study of war leads to these convictions:

---

* The February 1962 edition of the US Army Field Service Regulations (FM 100–5) does not contain this statement. It is, by the way, a far more sophisticated version than any of its predecessor Regulations and, incidentally, more so than any comparable publications of other services.

1. The destruction of the enemy's military force is the leading principle of war, and for all positive action the main way to the object.
2. This destruction of the enemy's force is principally effected only by means of the engagement.
3. Only great and general engagements will produce great results.
4. The results will be greatest when the engagements are united in one great battle.
5. It is only in a great battle that the general-in-chief commands in person. . . .

From these truths a double law follows, the parts of which mutually support each other; namely, that the destruction of the enemy's military force is to be sought principally by great battles and their results and that the chief object of great battles must be the destruction of the enemy's military force.*

It has long been a practice for writers on military strategy to quote Clausewitz, and his writings are so probing and inquiring and perceptive that he has mused on nearly all aspects of politico-military policy and relationships. And, in a fashion that would do credit to any scholar, he has looked at all sides of his problem. Unfortunately he died before he finished, and his unorganized notes and articles were posthumously published as a finished product. They are actually far short of that.

The result is that one can support nearly any side of any argument by citing Clausewitz. Most students of the past century and a half, however, have fastened on those more forthright portions of which the preceding quotation is typical. The quotation from the mid-50's Field Service Regulations— "The ultimate objective . . . is the destruction of the enemy's armed forces"—is a succinct indication that this theoretical

---

* Clausewitz, *On War* (Random House, Modern Library, 1943), p. 208.

basis has, in fact, been reflected in practice up to the middle of this century.

This is not a theory of strategy in quite the same sense that the sailor has his maritime theory or the airman has his air theory. It is much less complex than that. It is, however, a basic concept of warfare, and appreciation of these underlying factors could do much toward helping the nonsoldier understand why the soldier thinks as he does.

It may explain, for instance, the soldier's tacit (and sometimes not too tacit) opinion that air and naval forces exist primarily to transport the soldier to the scene of action and support him after he gets there. The soldier views the enemy army as the prime focal point of war, and all else should properly be subordinate. The soldier is impatient with the navy when the navy finds tasks that might interfere with taking the soldier where he wants to go, where the enemy army is, and keeping his supplies coming steadily. He is impatient with the airman who wants to put a machine tool factory out of business; he wants the airman to work on the enemy tank right across the valley from him. And the soldier, few men realize, is the only one of the military men who cannot do his part of the war alone. The airman can have his duels in the air and can bomb factories or enemy missile launchers or whatever he chooses all by himself. He does not need the soldier or the sailor to help him. The sailor can sail away and sink the enemy ships and control the seas and even extend his influence ashore, all with his own ships and his built-in air strength and his own specialized troops in the naval service.

But the soldier cannot function alone. His flanks are bare, his rear is vulnerable, and he looks aloft with a cautious eye. He needs the airman and the sailor for his own security in doing his own job.

This may give some further insight into the soldier's concept of strategy as this affects his ideas of organization for war. In order to do his own job best, the soldier feels he should control the forces that must function in his support. Thus we can understand the German organization in both world wars in which the soldier was supreme, and we can understand the steady insistence of the soldier's influence in this country—the slow movement toward some sort of a single national military staff, and the NATO and US organization in Europe today, where the supreme commander in Europe has organizational control of his sea flanks and his air overhead.

Whether for better or worse has been often debated. There is much in this line of argument that is well nigh irrefutable; but there is much that might be questioned, too. Is it, in fact, an always valid assumption that the ultimate objective of military operations must be the destruction of the enemy's army? The Japanese army was essentially intact and the great bulk of it undefeated in 1945. The catastrophe of Dienbienphu involved only a small portion of the total French army in Indochina; in that case the communists were given the victory because the people at home in France were shocked into throwing in the military sponge for political reasons. The airman and the sailor, and the politician too, from their different intellectual points of departure, may be expected to give careful scrutiny to this basic assumption of the soldier.

It has been the sailor, with some help from the airman, who has questioned the soldier's concept of organization. It was this basic difference of concept that gave rise to the heated defense organizational arguments of the late forties and the fifties in the United States.

The soldier, unable to carry out his war alone, felt that a centralized and unified national command structure was necessary to ensure efficient and effective support for armies overseas. The sailor, much less dependent than the soldier on outside help, felt he could do his sailor's job in a maritime situation more effectively and efficiently without the organizational intrusion of other services into his, the sailor's, business. And in doing that, the sailor argued, quite correctly, that he has never failed to meet the soldier's need.

The airman was torn both ways. The "tactical" air element was in a situation comparable to that of the soldier. He needed his supplies brought to him, and he needed his bases defended. In this, the airman thought like the soldier. The "strategic" air element, on the other hand, needed no outside help to do its job, and its intuitive gropings were for organizational autonomy, which is in keeping with the Douhet concept.

Fortunately, neither extreme position has been adopted and the resolution of the problem, the corporate joint body of the service chiefs, goes far toward meeting the needs of all the services.

The problem is that of deciding when and where and under what circumstances which basic patterns of thought can most profitably be put to practice. The problem is how the composite military mind can best make up its mind.

And that problem is today made appreciably more difficult by the emergence in practice of a new theory of war. It does not fit any of the classic rules; it does not even function in the same recognized arenas as the classic organized armies and navies and air forces. This new warfare is the "war of national liberation," as its proponents call it. And this very name, while it may not be accurate, is a most important clue as to its nature.

IV. THE MAO THEORY

The "war of national liberation" is usually referred to as guerrilla warfare, but that is too restrictive and misleading to use as a descriptive title.

Guerrilla warfare is not new. The word guerrilla itself came out of Spain in Wellington's despatches in the Napoleonic

Wars, but guerrilla actions are as old as history. There is no novelty in this.

But the current theory and the current practice are new. Mao Tse-tung is the father. Ho Chi Minh and Vo Nguyen Giap and Fidel Castro and Che Guevara are the able disciples and propagators of the faith.

The bibles (in English translation) are *Mao Tse-Tung on Guerrilla Warfare* by Brigadier General Samuel B. Griffith, USMC (Ret), which contains General Griffith's excellent translation of Mao's *Yu Chi Chan* of 1937; *People's War People's Army* by Vo Nguyen Giap; and *Che Guevara on Guerrilla Warfare* by Major Harries-Clichy Peterson, USMCR, which contains Major Peterson's translation of Guevara's *Guerrilla Warfare*, written in 1960 as a primer for Latin-American revolution.

These are all translations of communist books by very able communist writers who had put their communist theory to practice. And because the practice was successful, the books, and more importantly the theory, are inestimably important to every strategist, uniformed or civilian, in the Western world today. These books are not only theory, they portray a hard reality of contemporary warfare.

Before going further, one important point should be noted. While this theory is communist theory, it is not Russian communist. It is Chinese communist. And there is a fundamental and crucial difference.

Marx and Lenin and Stalin and Khrushchev all had a communist theory based on the urban proletariat. Marx started it by singling out the urban workers who were caught up in the Industrial Revolution. Lenin used the urban proletariat theory as the basis of his revolution, which was focused in the cities in order to gain direct control of the centers of government. Lenin ran a street-riot type of revolution. Stalin and his lieutenants used the same theory wherever force was needed in addition to the Russian army to establish control of the European satellites.

Mao tried the Marx-Lenin type of revolution, and it did not work. There was no urban proletariat of the Western style. So Mao changed Marx's basic point of departure. Instead of using the urban proletariat as his base, Mao reworked the theory and used the rural peasant. Russian and Chinese communist theories have much in common, but they do have this fundamental difference, and this difference alone is so important that it could well be a root cause of the current bitter arguments between the two countries.*

Be that as it may, our interest today is in the Mao theory of the war of national liberation. It is a new type of revolutionary war, and it includes but "is never confined within the bounds of military action." That last clause is General Griffith's. He goes on, in his introduction to his translation of Mao, to say, ". . . its purpose is to destroy an existing society and its institutions and to replace them with a completely new state structure. . . . For this reason, it is endowed with a dynamic quality and a dimension in depth that orthodox wars, whatever their scale, lack." [p. 7]

The theory is really very simple. One starts with a small, puritanically fervent group of believers. The first step is the political indoctrination of an expanding core of believers in the country. Then comes an expanding guerrilla warfare combined with political, social, and economic warfare, with all of them directed against the incumbent government and its forces. As this grows with success, it may or may not be expedient to use the enlarged guerrilla cadres in organized and

---

* It could also be a cue to the ideological differences between the Soviet Union and peasant Albania, and to the difficulties in Cuba, where Castro-Guevara communism is drawn economically toward the Soviet Union but ideologically toward Red China.

more orthodox armies. Finally the whole countryside is in controlled and organized hostility toward the existing non-communist government; that government is beaten or collapses; it is replaced by the communist apparatus; and the war of national liberation enters on its more orthodox stage of an autocratic and despotic communism.

The important point, and the crux of the Mao heresy, is that the rural peasant is the base of power. This is a rural, not an urban, revolution, and the important action takes place out in the country, not in the cities.

There is no point here in attempting to set forth the details of how to conduct guerrilla warfare. But some key quotations from Mao and his disciples may be useful in giving a feel for this kind of warfare. Probably the most widely quoted is the one about the guerrilla being the fish that swims in the mass of the people. Others are equally revealing.

From Mao by way of Griffith:*

There is in guerrilla warfare no such thing as a decisive battle; . . . [p. 52]

In guerrilla warfare, small units acting independently play the principal role, and there must be no excessive interference with their activities. In orthodox warfare . . . in principle, command is centralized. . . . In the case of guerrilla warfare, this is not only undesirable but impossible. [p. 52]

The tactics of defense have no place in the realm of guerrilla warfare. [p. 97]

And from Guevara by way of Peterson:

The guerrilla is—above all else—an agrarian revolutionary. [p. 7]

* Samuel B. Griffith (trans.), *Mao Tse-Tung on Guerrilla Warfare* (Praeger, 1961).

51

He is a social reformer. He takes up arms in response to wide-spread popular protest against an oppressor. [p. 7]

Guerrilla warfare is a fight of the masses, with the guerrilla band as the armed nucleus. [p. 6]

We believe that the Cuban revolution revealed three fundamental conclusions about armed revolution in the Americas:
1. Popular forces can win a war against an army.
2. One does not necessarily have to wait for a revolutionary situation to arise; it can be created.
3. In the underdeveloped countries of the Americas, rural areas are the best battlefields for revolution. [pp. 3–4]*

And then these excerpts from the North Viet Nam experiences related in Giap's *People's War People's Army:*

. . . it was first and foremost a *people's war.* To educate, mobilise, organise and arm the whole people . . . [p. 27]

. . . in a backward colonial country such as ours where the peasants make up the majority of the population, a people's war is essentially *a peasant's war under the leadership of the working class.* [p. 27]

There was no clearly-defined front in this war. It was there where the enemy was. The front was nowhere, it was everywhere. [p. 21]

. . . it was necessary to accumulate thousands of small victories to turn them into a great success, thus gradually altering the balance of forces, in transforming our weakness into power . . . [p. 28]

. . . with the development of our forces, guerrilla warfare changed into a mobile warfare . . . our people's army constantly grew and passed from the stage of combats involving a

* Harries-Clichy Peterson, *Che Guevara on Guerrilla Warfare* (Praeger, 1961).

52

section or company, to fairly large scale campaigns bringing into action several divisions. [p. 30]

. . . in the early years of the resistance a certain underestimation of the importance of the peasant question. . . . This error was subsequently put right . . . when the Party decided . . . to make the peasants the real masters of the countryside. [p. 33]

. . . the peasants, making up the great majority of the population, constituted the essential force of the revolution and of the Resistance War. [p. 44]

Guerrilla war is the war of the broad masses of an economically backward country standing up against a powerfully equipped and well trained army. . . . Is the enemy strong? One avoids him. Is he weak? One attacks him . . . and by combining military operations with political and economic action; no fixed line of demarcation, the front being wherever the enemy is found. [p. 48]

. . . each person was a soldier, each village a fortress, each Party branch and Resistance committee a staff. [p. 97]

Not only did we fight in the military field but also in the political, economic and cultural fields. [p. 97]*

It is, of course, difficult to capture the meaning of a whole book in a few quotations, but these have been chosen to illustrate three important points.

The first is that Mao's theory of war has already been tested; and in China, in North Vietnam, in Cuba, and in Algeria it was successful. We are not, in this case, talking about an idea *in vacuo;* we are talking about reality.

The second is that this basing of the theory on the rural peasant rather than the urban proletariat is important. And it

---

* Vo Nguyen Giap, *People's War People's Army* (Hanoi: Foreign Languages Publishing House, 1961).

is important because the uncommitted areas of the world are not urban, they are peasant societies, in Asia, in Africa, and in Latin America.

The third point shown by these quotations is the almost complete oppositeness of the Mao theory and the Clausewitz or continental theory of organized and mechanized massed armies:

Clausewitz has stipulated "destruction of the enemy's forces . . . only by means of the engagement . . . only great and general engagements will produce great results . . . results will be greatest . . . in one great battle."

The 1955 Field Service Regulations: "The ultimate objective . . . is the destruction of the enemy's armed forces."

Mao: ". . . small units acting independently play the principal role," and "no such thing as a decisive battle."

Guevara: "rural areas are the best battlefield."

Giap: "The front was nowhere, it was everywhere."

It is important to note here that while the normal strategy of the continental or Clausewitz theory is a sequential strategy, a main weight of the Mao theory is based on a cumulative, not a sequential, concept. This may be one of the most important differences between the two, and it could be the most difficult one for us to adjust to in practice. The guerrilla part of the effort is a cumulative one. As Mao said, there is in guerrilla warfare no such thing as a decisive battle. The sequential part of the Mao strategy is the political part; it is clearly pointed toward its aim, and the cumulative guerrilla warfare operates in support of it. Stated another way, the problem is how do we oppose a cumulative strategy with a sequential strategy? Or must we, ourselves, develop some sort of cumulative strategy to oppose it?

For another illustration, take the Eisenhower quotation "for this concern [Mr. Churchill's political interest] I had great sympathy, but . . . I was particularly careful to exclude such considerations. . . ." Then contrast this classical attitude of the nonpolitical soldiery with that of Che Guevara saying, "The guerrilla is—above all else—an agrarian revolutionary . . . He is a social reformer."

And Giap saying: "by combining military operations with political and economic actions."

It would be interesting if some scholar were to take the time to contrast Clausewitz and Mao in thorough investigation, and it could be profitable to contrast our own current beliefs with those of Mao and Guevara. We could learn from this how better to combat their brand of communism.

The Mao theory does exist, its postulates are rooted in the reality for which it was designed, and it is important. We must take it into account in any inquiry into general theories of strategy.

CHAPTER SIX

THE LIMITATIONS OF EXISTING THEORIES

EACH OF THE three Western major theories of strategy—we will omit Mao for the time being and come back to him later—has a substantial content of validity. They do or may have a direct coincidence with reality under certain circumstances, and to that extent they are practical theories. It is precisely because of these validities, these practicalities, that there are such marked and sometimes heated arguments between their proponents. The airman proposes his course of action in full confidence that he is right, and he then assumes in extension that his action is the best. The soldier, in the same fashion, offers his opinion and his proposal in the soldier's confidence that his answer is the best one. At the same time the sailor watches these two in a sort of aggravated frustration, unable to understand why neither of the other two can see that the sailor's answer is the best of the three.

To be sure, this is a gross overstatement of what actually occurs, but so set out to indicate what seems to be a basic source of difficulty between the military minds at work today.

The trouble, by and large, is this: each of the three Western theories, consciously or unconsciously accepted by the proponents as their intellectual points of departure, is treated tacitly as a general theory of warfare. So regarded, it is automatic to assume that this or that particular pattern of thought should be dominant in any war situation. And with these three contending theories for each strategic situation that may develop, the clash of ideas is little short of inevitable.

The point of the whole business is that none of the three is, in fact, a general theory of warfare. They are specific theories, each valid under certain specific conditions and diminishing in validity as the limits of reality within which they function depart from the tacitly identified ideal on which they are predicated.

Recall, for a moment, the matter of the strategic bombers during the Korean affair in the early nineteen fifties. The opponents of the air theory said the Korean experience "proved" that strategic bombers were overrated. The heavy bomber supporters said that this was not so; Korea was the wrong war, in the wrong place, at the wrong time. And nearly everybody missed the point. The strategic bombers were then, as they are now, fully able to do their job. The only hitch was that the assumptions did not coincide with reality. The Korean War was real enough; it was the assumptions that were not valid for that particular reality. Whether the reality—i.e., the Korean War—was "right" or "wrong" was irrelevant.

There is as yet no accepted and recognized general theory of strategy. Such a general theory would have to meet very stringent requirements. It would have to be applicable to any conflict situation, any time, any place. It would have to be applicable under any restrictions or limitations that might actually exist or might be placed upon it. It would have to absorb within its conceptual framework the realities of the existing specific concepts of war strategy, the continental, the maritime, and the air theories plus the Mao theory, which has been proven within the limits of its assumptions. And with this enforced generality as one of its requirements for validity, it must at the same time not be so vague as to itself be formless and unusable as a basis for intellectual discipline in the practical evolution of a plan of strategy designed to meet a particular situation of reality.

There are basically two ways of constructing theories, and one pays a price for each. First, one may make a theory of elements that are tautologically impeccable. One may build up a theory of statements that clearly are logical, deductively related, and consistent. For example, one might say as a start in such a system that "the strongest military force always wins." This is a tautology because "the strongest" is ultimately defined as "the force that wins." The price one pays for such a system is that it cannot be applied to any real situation that we know of. It exists *in vacuo,* and must continue to do so unless and until the ideal situation on which it is predicated actually comes to pass and the theory is put to test under these ideal conditions. Consider, in illustration, the Second World War in Europe, after which the doubters condemned the Douhet theory as a failure and the disciples stated that their theory was never given a fair trial, that the air strength was diverted to inefficiency.

The second method is to build a theory that explains only empirical facts that have already occurred. This, in different forms, is what the continental and maritime theories do. The price one pays is that such a theory does not necessarily account for what *could* have happened but did not, and the theory cannot be applied to future events with consistent rigor. What will be attempted here is to postulate a general theory that draws on both of these. Future work will, of course, be needed to uncover defects and fill in empty spaces in any general theory. But, at the present time, if a general theory is to escape the fallacy of tautology or the limitations of past experience, it must be largely speculative. The speculative will be trimmed, altered, diminished, and corrected by future work. I make bold to propose a general theory only because the time is long past due for someone to make the first step, to set forth the ideas that others can criticize, reject, or improve upon.

The only concept that has yet been postulated which approaches these requirements is Liddell Hart's concept of the indirect approach. He discusses this concept (and it appears in many of his writings besides those directly addressed to this subject) primarily in terms of the continental theory although he emphatically rejects many of the prime tenets of Clausewitz. His general approach to the subject has been, in effect, to overlay the theory of indirect approach on top of the continental theory of strategy and suggest recasting of the latter based on the newly offered concept. At the same time he deliberately widens the area of applicability in extension of his own concept beyond the purely military arena by inclusion of some of the more apparent social activities related to war. The psychological component of war he deliberately embraces within his concept as an integral part of it. Less specifically but by unmistakable implication, he includes the economic and political activities of conflict within the concept of the indirect approach. His historical examples span time, place, scope, and character in a catholic inclusion of varied human ingenuity in war. He argues, in effect, that the strategist should unbalance the enemy's system, should make him expend energy to regain balance. Success is achieved by unbalancing him beyond recovery. The supreme success comes in unbalancing him beyond recovery without even having to fight. This is enough to make Clausewitz turn over in his grave; no wonder so many soldiers flatly rebel at Liddell Hart's ideas.*

He does not specifically recognize either the maritime theory or the air theory of warfare in any of his discussions that I

* One soldier who clearly does not rebel is General André Beaufre, in whose book, *An Introduction to Strategy* (Praeger, 1965), may be found a somewhat different, and interesting, development of Liddell Hart's concept of "indirect approach."

can recall. But the concept does seem to be applicable to these to about the same extent that it is applicable to the continental theory; indeed, it is an essential quality of the maritime theory. And it is interesting to note that, in its degree of sophistication, the Liddell Hart theory is much more receptive to the concepts of Mao than those of Clausewitz. (And please don't jump to the absurd notion that I am classifying Liddell Hart with communists; I am talking about intellectual processes, not political beliefs.)

However there seems to be a defect in the concept of the indirect approach as it is now postulated. The incomplete vocabulary of strategy as an intellectual discipline limits the communication of the central concept of indirectness. This concept, as it now stands, is formless. By this is meant that it does not have a clear structure; it is slippery, it is nebulous, it is loose, and it is difficult in its deliberate application to the reality of a specific situation. Indirection, in and of itself, is not necessarily something to be sought after and need not necessarily produce any result but diffusion.

This is certainly not Liddell Hart's intent, and one may sense quite clearly an unstated pattern of his thought and what might be called the target of the indirection. But it is hard to be sure that the form it takes in one's own mind is the same as that which has generated some of his brilliant writings of the past four or five decades.

Here it is appropriate to make one point clear. This criticism of the theory of indirect approach is based upon deepest respect for it as the most perceptive that has yet been postulated. The combination of interest in it and difficulty in discussing it conversationally or applying it to actual or hypothetical situations is, indeed, a major incentive in having taken on the study of the content of this book.

At this stage of the discussion we are about to start probing in the direction of another concept, and to do so in abstract argument and what, we can hope, are logical steps. Whether the result will, in fact, be an alternate to the "indirect approach" as a general theory of strategy, or whether it will be an extension and clarification of that theory, I am not sure. I do know it will not be in conflict with it. Since there is general validity in the Liddell Hart theory, any other statement of general theory must be compatible with it.

Before going on, that last sentence should be discussed for a moment because it brings out a difference between warfare and other social activities such as politics or economics. A few pages back the point was made that the four generally recognized strategic theories—the maritime, the air, the continental and the Mao theories—are not general theories. Rather they are limited theories with the limitations being determined by the different assumptions implicit in each of them (the air theory limited by the tacit assumption that destruction can be equated to control, the continental theory being limited by the assumption that armies will meet in great decisive battle, etc.).

The Liddell Hart theory, however incomplete it may be, does not have this sort of limiting assumption. It has a general validity, and any other statement of general theory must be compatible with it.

If any two theories of strategy are not compatible, then neither of them is a valid general theory. Both of them have, somewhere in their structure, a limiting weakness; and these limitations should be uncovered and identified in order to forestall attempts to apply the theory in situations where it will not work, in situations where the underlying assumptions do not fit the realities of whatever actual situation may be at hand.

The field of strategy studied as a social discipline may be the only one of the disciplines in which this is true. (The physical sciences are not relevant for comparison here; they deal in predictable certainties. The "social sciences" deal with people, not things, and there is a built-in unpredictability when people are involved.) Coexistence of incompatible general theories is possible in all the other social disciplines because there does not occur in these areas of human activity an enforced collision. There are in actual practice today several general theories of economics that are not compatible. There are general theories of politics and of sociology that are not compatible. There are religious theories (or beliefs) that will not gear with each other. The structures of the several general theories within these fields, their ideas, their actions, will not mesh. Free enterprise, socialism, and communism are not compatible ideas, and the areas of reality where they impinge on one another are turbulent; but these clashings do not necessarily invalidate one or another of the competing schemes, no matter what our personal opinions of them may be. John Locke and Marx are as politically opposed as one could imagine. Christianity and Shintoism and atheism are incompatible. Yet these general theories can and do exist in their respective applications to human activity with a validity that appears quite satisfactory to their practitioners.

The reason that this is possible is that these general theories of the other social sciences are "general" only to the limits of the culture within which they function. When we take up the problem of war strategies we find that they are, almost by definition, intercultural. Thus the meaning of "general" in discussing theories of strategy is much more broad than we find in politics or economics or the like. The general theories of the social sciences are not necessarily universal, but the general theories of strategy must be so. They must be applicable to any war situation whether the practitioner likes it or not, because there is always the chance that his opponent might like it and might be able to force the disliked portion into the conflict. The assumptions on which general theories of strategy are based must be truly universal ones that will coincide with reality no matter what that reality may turn out to be.

That last is a tall order. The lack of universality in the assumptions underlying the present four major theories of strategy keeps them from meeting the requirements for acceptance as general theories.

The continental theory of war, in the pure form of Clausewitz, has built into its pattern the assumption that armies must meet and one must be defeated in battle; and it has in its substructure the tacit assumption that maritime war, or maritime communications, or air war need not be governing factors to which the needs of battle on land may have to adapt. The classic illustration is that of the Napoleonic Wars. The several campaigns of Napoleon were both the stimulus for Clausewitz and the archetypical illustration of his theories. The downfall of Napoleon was brought about not because some opposing strategist overcame Napoleon at Napoleon's own game, but because the power of the maritime concept or theory was applied to the conflict and Napoleon lost control of the sequence of events.

The maritime theory has as a necessary ingredient of its pattern the assumption that maritime communications are a necessary element of influence in the conflict.

The air theory has as an essential, though tacit, assumption the premise that control of a people can in fact be exercised by imposition (or threat of imposition) of some kind of physical destruction, and that, furthermore, this can be imposed from the air.

The Mao theory is based on the assumption that rural masses exist and can be used as the base of revolution. There are other fundamental assumptions, too, for all of them; but these will serve in illustration.

In no sense do I mean to imply that any general theory could eliminate all the sources of the present intellectual disagreements between soldiers and sailors and airmen and civilian strategists. Certainly we should not want to. A breadth of opinion and perspective and belief is a requirement for continuing resilient vitality in any social organism.

The conflicts between these types of military minds are based on differing judgments, and usually they are all more or less well-founded judgments and conclusions. The recognition of a general theory that would fit compatibly over the specific ones would lend a degree of order to the consideration and resolution of conflicting opinions. Such an intellectually disciplined order does not now generally prevail, and I believe it could be more closely approached. The existing process is one of compromise based largely on a genuine mutual respect and in lesser part on acceptance of a mutually tolerable lowest common denominator. In some few cases it results in an emasculated mediocrity. It could be considerably improved upon if the contenders—and this includes civilian as well as uniformed strategists—were to find a rationale within which they could function with generally prevailing mutual understanding as to common aims, common paths, and commonly understood and accepted individual tasks toward a common end.

Probably this would not reduce appreciably the intensity of the annual scramble for a slice of the budget, but it might very well put the budget allocation on more stable terms than the roller coaster on which it has too often ridden.

And, in passing, it should be noted that the budget arguments (not infrequently referred to as "service bickering") are not inherently bad or wrong, as is too often assumed. They are, or could be, a very sophisticated vehicle for discussion of the merits and the applicability of this or that concept as applied to this or that situation. Since the dollar is a catalyst to transmute an idea into actuality, the budget debates are a most appropriate public forum for the public decisions on public policy.

CHAPTER SEVEN

ASSUMPTIONS UNDERLYING A GENERAL THEORY

THE IMMEDIATELY preceding discussion imposes, in effect, certain requirements of universality and specificity and structure and inclusiveness that must be met by any general theory of strategy. In order to keep this discussion geared to the business of war strategy, it might be well to anchor these requirements to war-strategy foundations. In purely theoretical argument this narrowing of the field would not be necessary, but our interest at this point is not only pure theory; it is war strategy—a general theory of war strategy. These foundations, as they relate both to the intellectual and operational considerations of this particular kind of strategy, can be expressed in terms of war-planning assumptions.

The planning phase of strategy is selected as a device for the exposition of this background, this foundation, because the evolution of a plan is the connection between the theoretical consideration of war and the conduct of war. It is the situation in which the strategist finds himself with a foot in each camp, so to speak, the one the conceptual or theoretical aspect of strategy and the other the combatant or practical aspect of strategy. The war plan is a link between the thought pattern and reality. It is a vehicle for conversion of an idea to a deed. It is the military mind in action. The planning process is the area in which the employment of deliberately disciplined and orderly patterns of thought by the strategist must meet the test of practical reality.

So, to set the foundations on which to erect the outline of a general theory of war, four basic assumptions are offered.*

The first assumption is that, *despite whatever effort there may be to prevent it, there may be war.* This smacks of a low grade historical determinism, to be sure, but it is not presented in that sense. Rather, there are two explanatory comments to account for its inclusion at the head of this list. This assumption is really no more than an acknowledgment of the reason for being of armed forces in peacetime. There is no other profession in the world except possibly the medical that would as sincerely welcome disappearance of its need from the scheme of human existence. The assumption that there will be war is in no sense a desire of war for war's sake. But the necessity for the military man to assume that there will be war is something that consistently and subtly irritates the civilian. The civilian comes to feel that study or preparation for war must somehow be advocacy of war, although the cancer specialist never runs the risk of being viewed as advocating cancer. There is really a sort of aura effect—war is brutal, inhuman and cruel, and one must be the same if one discusses it. Second, this assumption that there will be war should periodically be recalled by the strategist himself to ensure his focus on the realities of war as contrasted with some of the war games and flights of fancy that sometimes lead us so far afield in peacetime.

The second assumption is that *the aim of war is some measure of control over the enemy.* This is a deliberately general statement. It would be satisfying to state it more precisely, but

* Some of this discussion of assumptions appeared in different form in an article of mine in the U.S. Naval Institute *Proceedings,* Vol. 83, No. 8 (August, 1957), pp. 811–17. [Reprinted as Appendix C to this edition.— Ed.]

the more it is considered the more it appears that such precision would be unduly restrictive. The specific requirements for the kind and degree and intensity and duration and extent of control can be determined only when a specific situation presents itself to the strategist and has developed to a point where specific decision is possible. But in spite of these assertions as to the need of generality, the purpose of war is not a matter to be got past so easily. The aim of war is a difficult subject to tie down because, historically, wars have been fought for so many purposes. Most of the time when men discuss the purpose of wars, someone trots out the assertion that wars are a continuation of policy by other means.* The discussion usually then goes on to the assertion that war purposes are basically the same as prewar policy purposes except that the means of pursuit of the policies are somewhat more violent. This is a very pertinent piece of business to take up here since it does bring directly to the fore the matters of war and policy and war aims.

The "war is a continuation of policy" idea is the basis of a great deal of coordinated planning, with the foreign offices and the military departments putting their collective heads together at frequent and regular intervals. But is it really a good idea, this notion that policy continues on after the outbreak of war? Is war in fact a continuation of policy?

For us, I think not. War for a nonaggressor nation is actu-

---

* This phrase, "wars are a continuation of policy by other means," is the one that is encountered in lectures and articles and military college discussions. Unfortunately, it is not an accurate quotation. What Clausewitz actually wrote, on page 596 of the 1943 edition of the Modern Library translation, is "war is nothing but a continuation of political intercourse with an admixture of other means." He then, in the next few pages, makes a good case to the effect that military action must serve political ends. Few people will argue with this. It is not Clausewitz with whom I take issue here, but with the large number of his inaccurate interpreters.

ally a nearly complete collapse of policy. Once war comes, then nearly all prewar policy is utterly invalid because the setting in which it was designed to function no longer corresponds with the facts of reality. When war comes, we at once move into a radically different world. Even looking past a war, a postwar world really has very little resemblance to any prewar situation; and the more comprehensive the war, the more valid is this assertion. It is a fairly safe bet that no participant, even Russia, in World War II had any clear idea before the war started what the world would really look like after it was over.

Even in the "little wars" like the Korean conflict, there was precious little "continuation of policy" for either contestant. For us, it was certainly an abrupt reversal of policy, possibly because of some sudden realization that the preceding policy was a schizophrenic sort of business, quite generally lacking adequate contact with the reality of its environment. For the communists the Korean War was no "continuation" either, because if they had foreseen the war as it actually happened they would probably not have moved into South Korea in the first place.

But before getting ridiculously far out on a limb, I should concede that war can be looked on as a continuation of a basic policy of national survival in one sense or another, no matter what the subpolicies toward survival may be. In that sense the continuation aphorism does have some validity; but in anything more specific than ultimate survival it would be prudent to apply far more critical examination than has been customary. Blind acceptance can lead us up some strange and dark alleys if we are not careful.

It might perhaps be safe to generalize by saying that for an aggressor, the one who starts a war on purpose, there may be a sizable element of continuity between the prewar policy and the war policy. This, for instance, is an accurate statement with respect to the communists in Vietnam and in Cuba. For the conservator, the one who is attacked, the coming of war is in most cases a dismal collapse of policy.

But because it is a collapse, it need not be a surprise. That is a different matter entirely, and forethought and planning need not be hampered. The relevant requirement is that reality be recognized. We should not expect to go merrily along in the comfortable delusion that our policies in a prewar world will have much resemblance to the facts of life in a war or a postwar situation.

Before leaving the assertion that the aim of war is some measure of control, there are two other relevant matters that should be touched upon. One concerns a traditional belief, and the other relates to what might be described as the purpose of the purpose.

The traditional belief, prevalent in just about every doctrinaire discussion that one encounters, is the Clausewitzian dictum that the aim—usually, by implication, the aim of the army—in war is the defeat of the enemy army. While there may be a good deal of truth in this, it does not have the inevitability of sunrise. Unthinking acceptance has frequently let this aphorism function as a narrowing limitation to the vision of the military mind, blinding the strategist to the possibility that there might be some course of action other than the head-on collision of armies.

Liddell Hart has used this theme as the basis for development of his theory of indirect approach. As we have noted before, it may well be necessary to defeat the enemy army. It may even be necessary to defeat it to the last remnant. But if we always saddle ourselves with the self-imposed restriction that we must, no matter what, defeat the enemy army in combat, then we have indeed denied to ourselves consideration of a vast span of actions that might more readily and easily achieve the needed measure of control.

The remaining item relating to the "control" assumption is the matter of its focus, its purpose. This subject reaches into the sphere of both the political philosopher and the philosophic politician—which is as good a definition of a statesman as any—and the sailor should tread warily here. So I will say only that the control sought in war should be neither so extreme as to amount to extermination—this is probably a cultural value judgment of the writer, and might not be valid in the eyes of one from a less humane culture—nor should it be so tenuous as to foster the continued behavior of the enemy as a hazard to the victor, which in most cases would be no victory at all—vide Korea. In general, most of us living within the ethic of Western culture could probably agree that the control achieved as victory should be adequate and appropriate to ensure that the enemy will regain status as a viable member of the world community, but in doing so will live and function acceptably within the framework of whatever may be the postwar world polity. Please note that much of this paragraph may be quite unwarranted from the communist point of view.

The third basic assumption for war planning is that *we cannot predict with certainty the pattern of the war for which we prepare ourselves.* We cannot, with reasonable certainty, forecast the time, the place, the scope, the intensity, the course, and the general tenor of a war. I think no man ever has. A strategy for an entire war is not predictable. This is particularly true with respect to the situation today, when we find ourselves faced by a potential enemy whose capabilities are not completely ascertainable and whose intentions are, in great measure, inscrutable.

When we accept the premise that we cannot forecast the pattern of war, nor its time nor its place nor its characteristics, then we arrive at the conclusion that the primary requisite in peacetime war planning is not a single rigid plan for war. Our first requirement, rather, is for a spectrum of war-plan concepts, for the broadest possible conceptual span of strategies for war, a spectrum that will embrace in both time

70

and character any war situation that might conceivably arise. The requirement is for a full bag of strategic concepts that will always provide, before and during war, not only a strategy applicable to a particular situation assumed for the future or existing at any given moment, but a most comprehensive reserve of strategies ready for use whenever the situation changes or when a war fails to proceed in accordance with the plan in use.

The strategist should take up specific situations only after the requirement for provision of the spectrum of concepts has been met, and then only for one of two reasons. The first is for the derivation of logistic and material needs. This is a process in which the estimation of logistic needs is based on a series of less favorable situations chosen from the full span of conceptual possibilities and tempered by judgments as to probabilities, as to tolerable costs, and as to hazards if not accounted for in the logistic and readiness plans. The second reason for which the military mind addresses itself to specific assumed situations is on the occasions when there may in reality exist a set of circumstances wherein either the probability or the potential hazard is so great and so clearly marked that specific and realistic plans can in fact be drawn on the basis of those assumptions.

Recent game theories* have sharpened one aspect of this. The player who plans for only one strategy runs a great risk simply because his opponent soon detects the single strategy—and counters it. The requirement is for a spectrum of strategies that are flexible and noncommittal, a theory that by intent and design can be applied in unforeseen situations. Planning for uncertainty is not as dangerous as it might seem; there is, after all, some order in military as well as in other

---

* *Theory of Games and Economic Behavior* by John von Neumann (John Wiley Science Editions, 1954) and *Strategy in Poker, Business and War* by John McDonald (Norton, 1950).

human affairs. But planning for certitude is the greatest of all military mistakes, as military history demonstrates all too vividly. There is always in mind the hazard of the Maginot mentality, ashore, afloat, airborne, or chairborne.

To resume the statement of the basic assumptions, there is offered as a fourth basic assumption for strategic planning foundation the following: *The ultimate determinant in war is the man on the scene with the gun.* This man is the final power in war. He is control. He determines who wins. There are those who would dispute this as an absolute, but it is my belief that while other means may critically influence war today, after whatever devastation and destruction may be inflicted on an enemy, if the strategist is forced to strive for final and ultimate control, he must establish, or must present as an inevitable prospect, a man on the scene with a gun. This is the soldier.

Of these four assumptions I think the first three are critical. Their acceptance and recognition, the latter as important as the former, are necessary for continuance of the argument. This fourth one—that the soldier on the scene is the ultimate determinant—is subject to considerably differing opinions. The Douhet theory in its pure form is predicated on the directly opposite assumption. Indeed, without such an implicit denial of the need for the soldier, the Douhet theory comes very near to collapse. I do not claim that the soldier actually on the scene is a requisite in every case; but I do believe he must be potentially available, and clearly seen as potentially available, for use as the ultimate arbiter. The war in the Pacific was actually decided before any soldier set foot in the Japanese home islands. But it was not decided until his ultimate presence there was inevitable unless the Japanese surrendered before he arrived. In a somewhat comparable situation, Malta was as starved and battered as any part of Japan. In the case of Malta, however, the presence of German or Italian soldiers never reached a state of inevitability. The soldier on the scene was never in sight. And Malta was never brought under control and never surrendered.

It may be that this fourth assumption, concerning the actual or potential presence of the man on the scene with a gun, can be rejected without fatal damage to a general theory of war. I do not at this time believe it can or should be rejected as a practical matter. It appears to me to be necessary unless and until there is brought forth some argument more compelling than simple assertion to the contrary.

CHAPTER EIGHT

THE DEVELOPMENT OF A GENERAL THEORY

A T THIS STAGE of the argument we find ourselves with four ideas relating to war and war strategy—that there will be war, that the aim of war is some measure of control, that the pattern of war is not predictable, and that the ultimate tool of control in war is the man on the scene with a gun.

What, then, are the general patterns of wars? How does one describe a war in general terms? I believe it can be done briefly something like this.

As far as an aggressor is concerned—and I use this word without the emotional and moral connotation that usually comes with the suggestion of aggression—as far as the aggressor is concerned the pattern of war consists of his attempts to establish and maintain, primarily by military means, a measure of control over the conservator* sufficient to force the conservator to conform to whatever may be the aggressor's terms. If the aggressor is successful in establishing some interim degree of control (which he is fairly sure of doing else he would not have dared start), then he either presses on to his victory or he is restrained somewhere in the course of the

---

* Again we have the problem of an inadequate vocabulary for theoretical discussion of strategy. I introduce the word "conservator" in this discussion because none of the words in normal use will fill the need.

74

war, and a sort of equilibrium sets in, a kind of inconclusive balance in which neither the aggressor nor the conservator is able to control the course of the war.

Before rounding out this model war, we should look at it from the conservator's point of view. For him, the pattern of war consists of an initial period in which he is beset by troubles, in which he is engaged in a tooth-and-toenail scramble to salvage as much as he can from falling under control of the enemy. If he fails to reduce the aggressor's initial control of the course of the war, he loses. If he is successful in first minimizing then neutralizing the aggressor's control of the course of the war, then there comes into being the period of comparative equilibrium that has been mentioned above.

It should be clearly understood that this term "equilibrium" does not mean a static halt to action, although it conceivably could be this. More probably it is a rather fluid and even dynamic state of indecisiveness in which neither side has a clear advantage and in which the minor advantages of both sides more or less cancel out in their cumulative effectiveness insofar as that relates to the control of the course of the war.

It is at this point, for both the aggressor and the conservator, that the critical decisions of the war are made. For the aggressor it is a question of whether to continue the pattern initially set by himself in the war, or to shift horses in midstream, so to speak, and start in a different strategic direction. The decision by the aggressor to alter the pattern after an equilibrium has set in is so rare as to indicate that this is a step almost beyond the reach of the military mind to conceive of and to carry out. Hitler's persistence in the face of rebuff indicates an extreme case of the deep-seatedness of this difficulty.

For the conservator, the arrival of the state of equilibrium is the occasion for a critical decision. It is a problem that can be stated very simply. Shall he continue to fight the war in accordance with the pattern initially set by the aggressor, a pattern in which the aggressor must be strong or he would not have selected that pattern to start with—or shall he deliberately take control of the pattern, shift the center of gravity of the war to a scene or to a character of his own choosing, and continue the war in this newly chosen and newly imposed pattern?

Before going further we should note that, in this description of war in the abstract, the aggressor-conservator classification has been used simply as a convenient device to indicate the two general extremes of the patterns encountered. A median position could, of course, be illustrated either by a war that starts by mutual consent or by a war that comes about by accident with both parties surprised to find themselves shooting at each other. In such situations, if one of them did not early seize and hold control and win the war, the same state of fluid equilibrium would come about. Both contenders would be faced with the fundamental decision as to whether and how to seize control of the course of the war by manipulation of the center of gravity to some scene or area or type of activity that would upset the equilibrium and tip the scales in favor.

The basic problem facing the strategist throughout all these situations, throughout any war, any time, any place, is this: Where shall be the center of gravity of the war? Shall it be where the opponent wants it for his purposes, or where the strategist wants it?

The conscious (or probably more often the unaware) capacity to recognize and act on this as the central problem of warfare is the difference between an Alexander or a Scipio or a Sherman or a Churchill and the multitude of lesser men in war.

It should hardly be necessary to elaborate on the incalculable value—military, political, psychological, economic, or what have you—that accrues to the strategist who is able to shift the governing weight of a war from the enemy's chosen location to a scene of his own choosing. (And it should be emphasized here that use of "center of gravity" and "scene" and similar words is part of the vocabulary problem mentioned early in the discussion. These words are not limited to the geographic connotation; the sense of these words is intended to include the qualities, tenors, and characters of war as well as its geographical locales.)

Control of the strategic weights or centers of gravity in any war, large or small, limited or unlimited, is a basic advantage that should be sought by any strategist. It is the fundamental key to the conduct of warfare.

In establishing and exploiting control of the pattern of war by manipulation of the center of gravity, there must be clear understanding in the strategist's mind as to the direction in which this center of weight is headed and the effect it will have on arrival. Furthermore, it must be a point at which the opponent is more than casually sensitive. Ideally, it should be some kind of a national jugular vein. At the least it should be in some sense neuralgic and one that will loom large enough in the opponent's structure to force accommodation to the strategist's own pattern in the manipulation of control. Oversimplified, the centers of weight of war should be moved by the strategist toward those points within the opponent's structure that are most critical to the opponent and are, at the same time, most vulnerable. In practice, of course, these two optimal requirements can seldom be met to their fullest, but the strategist's control of the war approaches completeness as these two ideals are approached in practice.

So it is proposed here that a general theory of strategy should be some development of the following fundamental theme: The primary aim of the strategist in the conduct of war is some selected degree of control of the enemy for the strategist's own purpose; this is achieved by control of the pattern of war; and this control of the pattern of war is had by manipulation of the center of gravity of war to the advantage of the strategist and the disadvantage of the opponent.

The successful strategist is the one who controls the nature and the placement and the timing and the weight of the centers of gravity of war, and who exploits the resulting control of the pattern of war toward his own ends.

This short discussion is not geared to historical analysis in the classic style, but a few moments of reference may serve to indicate a little more clearly what is meant. In *A Greater than Napoleon,* Liddell Hart has written a superb tale of Scipio Africanus and his strategic genius in the defeat of Hannibal and Carthage, and Liddell Hart illustrates his concept of the indirect approach in the maneuvers of these great captains.

For our purpose, looking only at the broad span of the actions over several years: Hannibal was firmly settled in Italy, and a succession of Roman generals had been unable to drive him out. Hannibal retained control of the pattern of those campaigns. When Scipio succeeded to the Roman command, he first moved the center of gravity from Italy to Spain, sailing there and taking control of Hannibal's source of men and supplies at Cartagena. His next major step was to move the main weight of the war to the African shores near Carthage itself. This touched a very sensitive Carthaginian nerve, and Hannibal was forced to conform to the pattern Scipio had set. He brought his Carthaginian forces back from Italy to Carthage. Scipio then shifted the pressure point of the struggle away from Carthage, where his enemy had grown strong, back up the valley whence Carthage got its food. Hannibal was forced to conform to this new move and, under the circumstances created by Scipio, was forced to meet Scipio on ground of the latter's own choosing. The Roman victory at Zama was fatal to Carthage.

The entire panorama of the duel between these two great men is a classic in the manipulation by the victor of the strategic center of gravity of the war. Scipio selected, in turn, the three points at which Hannibal and his Carthage were successively vulnerable, the three points of pressure that would force Hannibal to accede to Scipio's pattern for the war: from Hannibal's base to Hannibal's city to that city's granary. Hannibal had no choice but to fight the war as Scipio wanted him to. When the crucial turn came, it came on Scipio's chosen pattern.

A hundred years ago, a war was fought for three years in a more or less fluid state of comparative equilibrium, an equilibrium maintained by the less powerful Confederacy because it was able to set the pattern of the war—or, perhaps more accurately, because the Union did nothing to take control of the pattern of the war. The main weight of the war remained in northern Virginia more by default than by any design. The Confederacy had little choice but to hold the war there once the effort to move it north had failed at Gettysburg; and the Union seemed content to accept that area as the scene for its own center of interest and weight.

Finally, Grant applied some pressure in the West and a subsidiary center of weight was established along the Mississippi. Sherman* exploited this opportunity and, notwithstanding the continued activity in Virginia, the real center of gravity of the war moved over the mountains with Sherman into the heart of the Confederacy. Sherman manipulated the center of weight of the war as he marched. The pattern of the war was as he set it from then on. The surrender at Appomattox was brought about by the action of Sherman in the South far more than by the action of Grant in the North.

It was Sherman who manipulated the center of gravity of the war toward and then through the most sensitive and vulnerable area of the Confederacy. His actions controlled the

---

* Again it is Liddell Hart to whom we turn. His biography of Sherman is far and away the best of the many on this man and his strategies.

course of the war from the time he started across the mountains to its conclusion at the country crossroads.

In a survey so brief as to make a historian shudder, no attempt has been made to correlate the sequential strategies of the armies on land to the corrosive effect of the cumulative strategy of the Union blockade, an effect so gradual as to be difficult to identify at any particular instant. In most general terms, however, we can say that Sherman's campaign would not have been possible two years earlier, before the cumulative effect of the blockade, the war at sea, had begun to make itself severely felt in terms of the diminished resilience of the Confederacy.

As we look at the complete picture of the First World War, a somewhat comparable pattern emerges—with one major difference. The initial pattern of the war was set by the Germans with the center of gravity almost on a direct line between the geographic nerve centers of the opponents. Since the Germans were in control before the equilibrium set in, the scene as it settled down was much closer to the Allied sensitive areas than to the German ones.

In only two instances during that entire war did the Allies make any move whatever toward taking control of the pattern of the war. One abortive attempt took place at the Dardanelles, and the magnitude of that tactical fiasco was so great as to obscure its potential strategic importance for a full generation. The "might have been" in war is a slippery subject indeed, but this one is so beautifully illustrative that it should not be passed by.

If the assault on the Dardanelles had been planned and carried out with even a glimmer of organized tactical competence against the negligible resistance initially present, there might well have been three major results.

Russia might have been helped over her critical period of collapse, and something other than communism might have come out of the Russian chaos.

80

A new center of gravity would have been established in Germany's vulnerable rear areas, and Germany would have been forced to accommodate to this newly imposed pattern of the war—with what result, of course, no man can tell. Her allies in that area were wavering; she would have been forced to fight in an area not to her liking; and she was economically and politically as well as militarily vulnerable from the Balkans and the Hungarian granary.

And third, a success in the Turkish Straits might just possibly have opened the eyes of the maritime power of the West to the wide-open Baltic approaches to the heart of Germany. It is almost inexplicable, in retrospect, that this war could have gone on so long without someone's making an effort to upset the pattern of the war initially imposed by the Germans and accepted so blindly throughout the war by the ever-stronger Allies in the West.

Other than the futile move in the Dardanelles, the only noteworthy weight in the war outside of France itself was in the establishment of Allied control of the seas and the imposition of the maritime blockade. This cumulative strategy, as it had in America sixty years earlier, had its ultimate crippling effect. Indeed, since a sequential strategy comparable to Sherman's was never devised to take marked advantage of it, the economic (and thus political and social) strangulation of Germany is more and more generally recognized today as a crucial force that made victory eventually possible through the mud and the trenches of the Western Front.

In taking up World War II, we can look upon it, for our purposes, as three separate wars taking place simultaneously. Except for two instances—the deliberate decision by the Western Allies to keep the main weight of the war directed against Germany rather than Japan until Germany was defeated, and the inevitable conflict of interests in Germany between her western and eastern fronts at the end of her struggle—there was not too much critical interrelation be-

81

tween the wars in western Europe, in Russia, and in the Pacific.

In the war in western Europe, Germany moved much farther and much faster before the fluid equilibrium set in than in World War I, when Germany was held fast on and over the Channel.

As far as this war in Europe was concerned, the first battleground of our choosing was in northwest Africa in late 1942. It was at this point that the Western Allies took charge of the strategic pattern. Centers of gravity were established and in most cases well exploited in Sicily, in Italy, and then in Normandy—centers of gravity whose placement, timing, and weight were controlled to the advantage of the West. A subsidiary center of gravity in the air was moved from Britain and the Channel first to France and then to Germany.

From a far less favorable initial position and against a considerably more powerful Germany, the West was able to finish off the war in Europe with strength to spare.

In the war in Russia, the Germans' initial control of the war gave them almost incredible success before the first period of equilibrium set in. Once that had come about, the Russians were able to hold on and, liking the pattern of the brawl into which that war had degenerated, were content to keep to the existing pattern. Except for an occasional move or two, the Russians relied on main strength and manpower, and, on the other side, Hitler managed consistently to nullify the considerable tactical brilliance of several of his generals. There is not much, strategically, to be learned from the war in Russia except that it would be an uncommonly profitless business ever to duplicate. The cost per acre, to both sides, was appalling. It was a long, long walk from Berlin to Moscow and back again. That has been demonstrated more than once.

In the war in the Pacific, which was a maritime rather than a continental war, the pattern was initially set by Japan in her move to the southern archipelago. An equilibrium of sorts was established when the Americans held in the Solomons and New Guinea (largely by virtue of the victory at Midway a couple of thousand miles away) and, at the same time, the Japanese decided more or less indirectly not to push on and take control of the Indian Ocean and its entire littoral.

At this point, in 1943, we took charge of that war and shifted the main center of weight from Southeast Asia and the East Indies to the Central Pacific. There was a sort of sub-center in the Southwest Pacific, to be sure; but the main center of gravity of the war was in the Central Pacific, and it was pointed first westward to the Asian coastline to sever Japanese communications with her raw materials and then straight at the heart of the Empire. Once we put a center of pressure in the Central Pacific Islands, we held and manipulated control of the pattern of that war to its end.

Perhaps from these illustrations can be sensed something of what is meant by manipulation of the center of gravity and control of the pattern of war.

CHAPTER NINE

OBSERVATIONS ON THE APPLICATION OF THEORY

So if this postulation of a general theory of strategy does have substance and validity and practicality, it might be able to provide a common and basic frame of reference for the special talents of the soldier, the sailor, the airman, the politician, the economist, and the philosopher in their common efforts toward a common aim.

If we examine the four major limited theories of strategy—the continental, the maritime, the air and the Mao theories—and add to them the broader Liddell Hart theory of indirect approach, we find that they will all fit within the postulated general theory to the extent that the assumptions of the limited theories mesh with the realities of whatever may be the situation at hand.

Illustratively, if there is a rural peasantry and it can be subverted to communist control, then the Mao theory of wars of national liberation will fit within the general theory. If the war situation is such that massive destruction would achieve some measure of the sought-for control, then the air theory—or whatever may be its modification as aerospace theory—will fit within the general theory, and the latter can provide a context and a focus within which to apply the former. If maritime communications and control are a factor within the problem, to that extent the maritime theory and maritime forces are relevant and can be applied within the general concept. And to the extent that modern massive armies are relevant to the situation at hand, then to that extent the concepts of the continental theory are valid and usable within the total scheme.

This brief and abstract summary of the two preceding paragraphs opens the way for three observations that are relevant to the construction or planning of a strategy.

First, I have said that if the assumptions of a limited theory coincide with reality, then the theory is applicable. By turning the coin over, so to speak, perhaps we could exclude from the conflict some key element of an opponent's strength by deliberately keeping one of his specific assumptions from becoming reality.

Let us look at the Korean action of 1950 in this light. The communists gave us our "air sanctuary" by not attacking our air bases in the rear and afloat. Our acceptance of this implied a quid pro quo, and we excluded our strategic bombers from major participation. We did not bomb across the Yalu. Or perhaps it was the other way around. Perhaps we did not bomb across the Yalu, and they did not attack our fleets at sea. At any rate, both sides did this knowingly, and knew what they were doing and why. This exclusion is what kept the strategic bombing component of the air theory apart from the existing reality of the situation—i.e., the "wrong war," it did not fit the assumptions on which the strategic bomber concept was predicated—and it kept the full force of the Strategic Air Command out of the Korean conflict.

In another illustration, the Mao theory depends on getting control of the rural peasantry. One of the things we have tried to do in South Vietnam is to invalidate a basic assumption of the Mao theory. The "strategic hamlet" program of about 1963, for instance, was aimed at preventing communist control of the peasantry. No water (people) for the fish (guerrilla) to swim in. This action, the forestalling of communist control of the peasantry, is the one thing the French did not do a decade ago in what is now North Vietnam. If an appreciable proportion of the rural peasantry cannot be brought around to the revolutionist's side, the war of national liberation cannot get off the starting blocks.

And while no one has deliberately taken action to invalidate an assumption in Laos, this same line of reasoning may shed light on difficulties in that situation. This is one of the few places in the world where we are confronting the communists in a place that we cannot reach by sea. There is no direct maritime access to Laos, and for that reason many of the direct and indirect assets of our maritime strength cannot be applied to the Laotian problem. There are not many other such places where the maritime element of our national strength cannot be applied, but where this is true, where the underlying premises of the maritime concept are not directly applicable, the problem is much more difficult. The other elements of our national strength must be adjusted to compensate for the partial exclusion of the capabilities normally derived from the maritime. As a hypothetical illustration, let us assume a conflict involving us in Afghanistan. Air transport, air drops and landings, and air support would have to do not only their own jobs but those of the sailor too.

In a not so hypothetical illustration, in 1939, Great Britain, the maritime power, offered a guarantee to support Poland in the face of threat from Germany, the continental power. Poland was not accessible by sea in that situation and, regardless of the moral or political strength of the British guarantee, the reality of the Polish situation did not include the basic premise that would have let British maritime strength play a role.

From this it would appear that a fairly careful scrutiny of the opponent's thought patterns and their underlying assumptions should be an early component of our own planning process. If we could deliberately make his theory invalid, we have gone a long way toward making his actions ineffective. An examination of this type might uncover something crucial in reaching toward establishment of control.

It is this word "control" that brings up the second observation. This is the matter of statistical analyses of the tools of war and their use.

During World War II a group of techniques known as "operations research" furnished some exceedingly useful help in the employment of weapons and weapons systems, particularly in antisubmarine warfare in the Atlantic. Then after the war the concept of the application of statistical and other mathematical techniques was further developed and expanded to include not only operational employments but assessments and comparisons of basic values of various tools of war. In the years following the war, it was applied first, and very successfully, to analyses of various aspects of the air problem— penetration prospects, defense prospects, damage expectancies, and the like.

Because it was so efficient and useful a technique, it was expanded even further in a series of brilliant managerial developments as an aid in determining the relative values of entire systems and combinations of systems. "Cost effectiveness" became a cornerstone of defense management and budget determinations.

The system worked beautifully with respect to aircraft and missiles and air defense and their warheads; but it ran into snags, and the results were a little less precise and less generally accepted when the "cost effectiveness" statistics were applied to other types of instruments of warfare. The soldier was uncomfortable trying to measure the cost effectiveness of an armored division, for instance, and the sailor had difficulty in accepting statistical measures of the worth of a ship or a group of ships. The process just would not work out into clean and precise figures as would the process applied to the air and missile bombing elements.

The soldier muttered and the sailor grumbled over this new managerial revolution, but no one seemed able to refute the statistics.

Perhaps here, too, the answer lies not in the techniques but in the theory. The air theory is predicated on delivery of destruction. Destruction is a finite and measurable phenomenon; so is the flight of a missile and the delivery of a bomb. But destruction is not so clearly the cornerstone of the continental and the maritime concepts of war.

The aim of the soldier is to establish control over the enemy by overcoming his army and thus destroying his will to fight. The aim of the sailor is to establish and exploit control of the sea and extend, by a variety of pressures, control from the sea onto the land, where the opponent is.

Destruction in each of these two cases is only one component of control, and not the whole of it. The soldier exercises his ultimate control by his unchallenged presence on the scene. The sailor contributes to control in part by destruction, but as much by other components. Like the soldier, in some cases, by his presence. Or, as often as not, by making possible various political or economic pressures toward control. The Sixth Fleet, for instance, is a political force of the first magnitude in the Mediterranean, and its day-to-day sailings are determined as much by diplomatic as by military factors.

How does one figure the cost effectiveness of the presence of a battalion in Berlin, or of a destroyer in the Persian Gulf? Control of this type, in its more sophisticated sense, is probably better described as "influence," but it is nonetheless a degree of control, and as such it is a legitimate and useful "purpose" in assessing the worth of these instruments of strategic policy.

The point to be made here is that the more sophisticated the strategic concept—and this need have no relation to the sophistication of the technologies involved—the more elusive are the statistical measures of worth. Destruction is measurable and can be mathematically forecast to a great degree; control is a matter of living people, and thus must, probably for a long time to come, remain a matter of human judgment. It is very difficult to put a statistical probability in one column and a human judgment in the other and compare them. We do not yet have the techniques for that except in another human judgment. It is the nature of the strategic theories that limits the application of the mathematical analyses in the management of the tools of war.

There is a third observation that may be derived from the interrelationships of the general and limited theories.

We have established the strategic aim as some measure or some kind of control; and we have stated that a general theory of strategy "should be able to provide a common and basic frame of reference for the special talents of the soldier, the sailor, the airman, the politician, the economist, and the philosopher in their common efforts toward a common aim."

The inclusion of these latter three along with the men at arms is, of course, deliberate. It is deliberate because control—direct, indirect, subtle, passive, partial or complete—is sought and exercised in so many ways other than military. Diplomatically it is exerted largely by mutual agreement. Economically it is exerted largely by self-interest and, in its most basic form, a desire to keep up the habit of eating. Philosophically the pressures and constraints of control are perhaps the most subtle and, at times, the most pervasive and persuasive of all.

Consider the amount of control exercised over the past two millennia by the philosophy of Christianity. Consider the control exercised today by the philosophy of communism. And by the philosophy of individual freedom.

This is what we seem somehow to have missed in our strategies for freedom in the rural-peasant societies of the world—in those areas where the Mao theory of "wars of national liberation" is, far and away, the most dangerous foe we have to face.

In some ways we have, intuitively, recognized the problem. The "strategic hamlet" program in South Vietnam is aimed at forestalling or making more difficult the communist efforts to provide the "water" for the guerrilla "fish." The Peace Corps seems to be headed generally along a roughly parallel path. But neither of these efforts seems to get at the root of the problem, which is the need for articulation of a philosophy to be "for."

This is not a suggestion that someone go out and think up a brand new religion or a brand new political scheme. But it is a suggestion that, at the least, we might do a better job of adapting what we have (which is very fine indeed) to the actual situations that confront us.

We have known for a long time that, in our society, the Anglo-American, two-party electoral system of applied democracy is both an efficient and an acceptable system for the allocation, use, and transfer of power, which is the basic problem of politics. And we have known, too, that it provides us a quite satisfactory context for observance of our predominantly Christian spiritual ethic.

But we have had a great deal of difficulty in stretching these two schemes of ours to fit other societies. Our basic, and usually tacit, assumptions have not often been in very close coincidence with those of the other societies that we have wanted to win over to our side.

If we could adjust the assumptions to fit the reality of the scene of action, we might get forrader faster.

It is a little difficult to give an illustration of what is meant in this abstract discussion of philosophic strategy because illustrations are so scarce—or because I am a sailor, not a philosopher. But two short ones may serve.

One is the way that Mao has rearranged the theories of Marx to fit the situation in China. Marx focused on the urban worker who suffered under the dislocations of the early days of the Industrial Revolution. This man did not exist in China, or at least did not exist in sufficient number to be a governing element of effective revolution. So Mao revised Marxian theory to focus on the rural peasant, and this revised theory has worked with chilling effectiveness in rural societies.

The other example is fictional, but it is nevertheless directly relevant to today's problem of what strategies we should use to influence the uncommited areas of the world toward us rather than toward the communists. Father Finian, in *The Ugly American,** went into a remote corner of Southeast Asia and helped the villagers devise a rationale, and, within that rationale, a plan of action designed in order to achieve the end of defeating the communists.

This fictional† Roman Catholic priest, and quite fittingly a Jesuit intellectual disciplinarian, devised a strategy firmly rooted in the reality of the scene of action; he put into effect his plan of action; and he achieved his end.

It is something like this that we need to serve as a sort of foundation on which to build the whole strategic rationale. We would not all agree that it need be based on Jesuit Catholicism, or perhaps even on any religious philosophy. But it must have an acceptable and locally viable philosophic base; and it must be a strategy suited to, rather than imposed upon, the actual scene. The fighters must believe in what they fight for. The basic assumptions must fit the reality.

---

* By Burdick and Lederer. You do not have to like, or to agree with, this controversial book. The point is that this episode in the novel is a brilliant adaptation of a philosophic rationale to a very real situation.

† Did the authors develop this piece of their fiction from the real Father Hoa in the southern tip of South Vietnam? If they did, then the illustration is all the more pertinent.

CHAPTER TEN

CONCLUSION

IN THESE LAST few paragraphs I have, for the first time, discussed strategies that are not military. I have been talking about strategies of philosophy-in-action, skipping purposely over the fields of politics and economics, where we are more accustomed to various kinds of conflict. This has been done for two reasons.

The first is to illustrate the assertion made early in this discussion: that strategy, by the definition we have used, is not limited to a war situation or to military application. A general theory of strategy should be applicable in any conflict situation.

And, second, to illustrate that the military problem is only rarely isolable from the total social context within which, and on behalf of which, it functions.

Some obvious examples of this corelationship today are in Cuba, in South Vietnam, and in NATO in Europe. Only in part are these military problems. The strategic theories for these, or any other, situations today must be able to encompass all, not just the military, aspects of power in reaching toward control.

To summarize, I started from the premise that there is not a good intellectual foundation for past and present strategic thinking and criticism; and I hope I have made the point that strategy is properly a matter for public attention, not only by officials of government but by the public at large and particularly by scholars who might usefully turn their talents more fundamentally and objectively toward the problems of the use of power.

Following that, to show where we stand today, there have been short expositions on the existing theories of military power, with comments on the limitations of these theories in their applications to the specific realities of given situations. And in discussing theories of military power I have stepped over into the field of the political philosopher by including the theory of Mao Tse-tung as a military theory. To find justification for this, one need only look toward Vietnam.

Then I have worked back and isolated one factor that is common to all power struggles, military or nonmilitary. This common factor is the concept of control, some form or degree or extent of control exercised by one social entity over another. As it relates to my profession, I have been talking about one form or another of military control. But I do hope that it has come out clearly that military control, or military affairs in the broad sense, can seldom be taken up in isolation. Military matters are inextricably woven into the whole social power fabric. And that is why a general theory of strategy must, I believe, be a theory of power in all its forms, not just a theory of military power.

In order to give form to theory, I have introduced the concept of the center of gravity, the focal point, in the application of power as the idea that supplies force and direction toward the concept of control—a purpose, together with a system of measures for its accomplishment. Control is the purpose, and the manipulations of the center of gravity of the situation are the measures for its accomplishment.

Finally, as I said in the preface, I am not the one to judge whether my speculations on a general theory of strategy will prove valid. But if they induce someone else either to refine and amend what I have offered, or to propose something different and better, this book will have served a useful purpose.

Some method of bringing intellectual order into strategy is long overdue.

TWENTY YEARS LATER

IN 1950, two of us[1] at the Naval War College were trying to plan a course of study on "why we need a navy." We needed something more penetrating than pounding the table and shouting "Of course we need a navy—any idiot knows that!" So we traveled up and down the East Coast asking perhaps two dozen university scholars how we might address this problem.

Most of them simply did not understand what we were groping for. A few tried to persuade us that the solution lay in their own discipline—history, economics, sociology, political science, or whatever.

But two of them gave us what turned out to be the same answer, and each did it in terms so abstruse that it took us a day or so to figure out what they had said. One was Professor John von Neumann, a mathematician at the Institute for Advanced Study at Princeton, New Jersey. The other was Professor Harold Lasswell, who was an economist turned soci-

---

1. The other was the late Eugene L. Burdick, then a Lieutenant Commander, Naval Reserve. After World War II he had gone to Oxford as a Rhodes scholar and, unlike most, had stayed to earn a doctorate in political philosophy, at the apex of the scholarly pyramid. When recalled by reason of the Korean affair, he had been teaching only graduate students at Berkeley. His was probably the best mind I have ever known.

ologist turned political scientist, and was then on the staff of the Yale School of Law.

What they had told us, each in his own fashion, was this: we needed a theory, and we needed a vocabulary with which to talk about it. With those two intellectual tools we could then address the problem of why we needed a navy.

That was the genesis of what turned out to be, several years later, this book. On page 11 I paraphrased the von Neumann–Lasswell ideas on how to address our problem: "With respect to strategy as a subject of study, its intellectual framework is not clearly outlined, and its vocabulary is almost nonexistent. These two primary tasks are badly in need of doing. . . ."

I wrote about the four existing theories of strategy, although few people had ever publicly recognized them as theories. I classified each of them as "specific" theories, valid only within the limits of the basic, and usually unstated, assumptions on which they were predicated. Then I turned my hand to devising a general theory of strategy, valid anytime, anyplace, and under any circumstances. And I invited anyone interested to alter or amend or replace it.

As far as I know, no one has ever paid any attention to it. I don't know whether this is because it is so clear and obviously valid that no one needs to, or because it is of no use at all. I suspect it could be the latter, but I really do not know.

Here it might be well to say again what a theory is, and in doing this I use the thought patterns of the physical sciences more than those of the social disciplines. A theory is an idea, a scheme, a pattern of relationships designed to account for events that have already happened with the expectation that this pattern will allow us to predict or foresee what will come to pass when comparable events take place in the future. It is never possible to "prove" that a theory will forever be valid. But it is always possible that a result may occur outside the pattern expected; in this case we must go back and either discard the theory or amend it to take account of what actually occurred.

I still think the postulated theory is a valid one, not yet disproved. So perhaps it might be useful to restate two paragraphs from pages 77–78:

> The primary aim of the strategist in the conduct of war is some selected degree of control of the enemy for the strategists's own purpose; this is achieved by control of the pattern of war; and this control of the pattern of war is had by manipulation of the center of gravity of war to the advantage of the strategist and the disadvantage of the opponent.
>
> The successful strategist is the one who controls the nature and the placement and the timing and the weight of the centers of gravity of the war, and who exploits the resulting control of the pattern of war toward his own ends.

This was purposely a very general statement. If we accept the premise that a strategy is a plan for doing something in order to achieve some known end, then it seems an adequately precise postulation. The aim of any strategy—land, sea, air, diplomatic, economic, social, political, a game of poker, or the way of a man with a maid—is to exercise some kind or degree of control over the target of the strategy, be it friend, neutral, or opponent. I have used the word "control" because I can't find a better. The vocabulary is not wholly adequate to the need. In many cases "influence" might be more nearly the word; less often it could even be "dominance." Take your choice, or find other words that better fit your situation. I have settled on "control" simply as an umbrella to cover the full span of possibilities.

In the case of maritime strategy (which was understandably my first interest), the aim is the extension of control from the sea onto the land. Note here that the more frequently discussed control-of-the-sea is a necessary prelude, a means, to this end. And remember also that the control extended from the sea onto the land, which is where people live, can be political, or economic, or psychological, or military, or any combinations of various pressures toward control. It can be direct or subtle, overt or covert, or immediate or slow or delayed in its working. And, again, some forms of it might be more accurately described as direct or indirect influence.

Probably the most slippery and least precise bit of this postulated theory has to do with "manipulation of the center of gravity," or control of "the nature and the placement and the timing of the center of gravity." Another way to say this is that the strategist needs some leverage to induce or force the other fellow to accede, wholly or in part, to what the strategist wants.

The President, seeking a particular piece of legislation from the Congress, may adopt a strategy in which his leverages include both a carrot (to induce) and a stick (to force) in hopes of reaching some mutually acceptable agreements.

The diplomat engaged in arms control or trade negotiations follows essentially the same path in his strategy.

The man a-wooing the maid uses as his leverage the carrot.

The armed force at war depends on the stick.

And that brings up another matter. The principal stick available to armed forces is some kind of destruction. The correlation between destruction and control, which varies widely from one situation to another, has been essentially neglected in public discussion of military strategy.

It is not too difficult for an army on a battlefield to resolve one aspect of this: just use a bazooka and destroy that tank. With one less enemy tank, the army is a little closer to control of the battlefield.

In my own profession, we can often use the same reasoning: sink a hostile ship or submarine and we are that much closer to control of that part of the sea.

The Air Force problem (and the Navy has some of this, too) quickly gets more difficult the farther it reaches beyond the battlefield. The tank shot up by a plane in "close interdiction" just substitutes the aircraft weapon for the bazooka. But what about the so-called "deep interdiction" and "strategic bombing"? How, and how much, do these destructions contribute to the control that is the aim of war? Monday-morning quarterbacks today still question the Dresden and Hamburg firestorms and (to my private fury since most of them were not then living, much less at risk) noisily question not only the need but the morality[2] of the Hiroshima and Nagasaki bombs.

Here let me clearly state that, by bringing up these matters, I am not automatically opposing "deep interdiction" or "strategic bombing," or opposing nuclear missiles in submarines or silos. These latter, by the way, are a quite separate subject. What I am trying to do is to indicate that this basic aspect of the use of armed force, which necessarily involves many different kinds and degrees of destruction, needs a lot more thought and analysis than I think it has had either in public or in organizational privacy.

What are the relationships, the correlations, between destruction and control? What will this show of force (which is potential destruction) or that segment of actual destruction contribute, directly or indirectly, now or later, to the control we seek as our aim in peace or war? Only by facing up to that kind of question, clinically rather than emotionally, can we move from profligacy toward efficiency in the planning and conduct of war. I am quite sure this matter needs attention.

Twenty years ago, in this book, I also tried in a very small way to expand the vocabulary. In addition to sliding in, unremarked, a few such words as "sequential," "cumulative," and

2. See page 15 to get morality in strategy squared away.

"specific" to describe types of strategic theories, I introduced a couple of words such as "conservator" to describe the opposite of "aggressor." No one has paid any attention to this either. More importantly, no one has come up with anything more acceptable. I still think we need such an antonym.

We do, in the U.S. armed forces, have a remarkable ability to create an almost revolting patois. For instance, with what must be dozens of ways to say that one does not agree, someone in the Pentagon came up with a new one. In my day, and probably even now, if one service does not agree with another's proposal, that service "non-concurs." Dreadful, isn't it? And really not the sort of thing we need to expand our intellectual grasp of ideas.

But there has been at least one small bit of progress. I understand that there has recently come into fairly general use the phrase "operational art" to describe that area in which there is a gap between strategy and tactics. If that fills a need, and apparently it does, then we are better off than we were.

But we still need a larger and more precise vocabulary with which to talk about, and thus to think about, our profession of strategy. Shakespeare, where are you when we need you?

To move from rather elusive abstractions to something more specific (see what I mean about vocabularies? "Specific" in this sentence has a different connotation from that a few paragraphs back), let us take up another matter.

In the fifties and sixties, when I was writing this book,[3] I tried to present it so that time and contemporary events were not essential elements of the ideas. If theories are to be valid, they must have a certain quality of timelessness. They must be relatively immune to being overtaken by events.

3. Much of the writing was done in the middle fifties when I was at sea in a single-screw low-speed amphibious cargo ship; an AKA is not as demanding of a captain's attention as is, for instance, a destroyer.

Now, twenty-odd years later, I think that time and technology, in two instances, make it necessary to modify what I then said. One of these has to do with cumulative strategies, and the other with control of the seas.

On page 27, discussing cumulative strategies, are these statements:

> . . . it is not implied that this operational-pattern concept can be systematized to the extent that it is susceptible to anything so concrete as rigid mathematical tabulations. . . . [Instead,] it is . . . a reference concept . . . Nothing more, I fear, than that.

Over the last two decades I have come to believe that cumulative strategies are probably more important and can be more accurately addressed than I then believed. I now think that the information-management revolution has probably made cumulative strategies more readily subject to analysis in planning before the events, in carrying out those plans, and in the retrospective analysis of what has already taken place. I refer, of course, to the advent of transistors, chips, hardware, software, and the whole apparatus of computer capabilities in the management and analysis of information. The techniques of just how this is to be done are quite beyond me. My scant electronic education petered out with vacuum tubes. But I do appreciate quite clearly that the data-management revolution of the past two or three decades has opened up new fields and new techniques of understanding.

I am certain that, in the strategies (or operational art?) of aircraft and missile employment, the advent of computer techniques has exponentially improved the planning, the conduct, and the analysis of results. Therefore I now sense that this particular form of cumulative strategy could be a far more predictable one, and thus a more precisely employable one, than it was some years ago. But it still functions within the limits of the assumption that destruction can be equated with control.

In like vein, a tonnage war at sea, another cumulative strategy, could be directed with more precision, and could be analyzed as it progresses, with degrees of understanding not available in the past.

With only a little less sense of certainty, I suspect that some of the less obvious forms of cumulative strategies could, with the newly available techniques of managing information, become more effective than in the past. I refer here to such matters as economic warfare, psychological warfare, some forms of covert warfare such as disinformation campaigns, and probably even diplomatic and political strategies, all of which are basically cumulative in their effects.

As for the second matter, that of control of the sea, its conduct, too, must be modified by other facets of the recent explosion of electronic capabilities.

On one side of the coin is the fact that the combat arena, the battle area at sea, has grown from horizon distance to many hundreds of miles. And on the other side is the fact that a ship out of sight of land is no longer invisible. The advent of missiles with combinations of remote guidances and homing capabilities has extended the battle areas. The advent of satellites and other search capabilities has extended the search to cover essentially all the world's ocean areas.

One recent illustration of the extension of the search and battle areas, although no shots were fired, was the fairly recent interception and capture of the *Achille Lauro* pirates when they were later flying out of Egypt.[4] What happened was that the Sixth Fleet ships and aircraft took under close

4. On 7 October 1985, the Italian passenger ship *Achille Lauro*, with 454 people on board, was hijacked by Palestinians. A U.S. passenger was killed before the ship came into Port Said on 9 October. An Egyptian airliner carrying the hijackers back to Tunis was intercepted by U.S. fighters on the 10th and forced to land in Italy. The Italian police held the hijackers, but PLO head Abbu Abbas, who negotiated their surrender, was allowed to leave.

surveillance the entire eastern half of the Mediterranean. In that enormous thousand miles from Malta to the Levant, they found and identified the one aircraft they were seeking. They diverted it to Sicily. And they did all this in darkness. This was probably the largest sea area that has ever been brought under complete and selective control for a single particular purpose.

That is the "plus" side of modern technology in control of the sea. A "minus" side is that no ship, and perhaps no aircraft, can long escape detection. The many varieties of sensors may, to a large extent, make it quite difficult for ships to move in secrecy. This will alter the tactical conduct of war at sea and may thus affect the strategies available for adoption.

I believe the sea power theory itself remains valid—the establishment of some effective degree of control and use of the sea in order to extend control onto the land. Here it is important to say again that there are many varieties and degrees of the control that is extended onto the land. This control may be military, or economic, or political, or psychological. It may vary from complete control to subtle shades of influence. And it may have its effect at once or it may take a long time to be felt. But the basic concept is still good.

I also believe that the techniques and the tools and the tactics of establishing and exploiting control of the sea will continue to undergo some rather marked changes. The expansion of the battle area, the advent of long-range weapons, and the improved capacities for surveillance are bound to continue to alter the methods that my generation grew up with.

There is another aspect of strategy that has come more to the forefront than it was twenty years ago when this book was published. This is the problem of terrorism in all its forms—murder, kidnapping, violent and selective destruction, well-publicized threats, and all of it planned for clever and effective exploitation of modern mass communications in

free societies. This latter, mass communications in free societies, is an indispensable element of terrorism. Closed societies, with control of mass communications, are not good
targets.

While generalizations are always chancy, it does seem that
the most persistent and lasting of these terrorist activities
have at their roots the intense and revolutionary nationalisms
that have emerged as part of the vast and worldwide social
revolution of this twentieth century. The extreme Irish, the
Palestinian, the Iranian, and the Puerto Rican groups are examples. More vaguely and more incoherently nationalistic,
and almost nihilistic, are such as the Bader-Meinhof and Red
Brigade groups in Europe. In the United States we have had
the Weatherman group and the preposterous Symbionese[5]
Liberation Army.

Among the many books on the subject (and the literature
on this matter has proliferated along with the fact), the best
and most succinct exposition of terrorism that I have encountered is by Robert F. Delaney, in an independent study course
designed to inform both police and industrial security person-
nel.[6] The following two paragraphs are condensed from it:

> Who are these politically activated persons whose alienation
> is so complete that they desire to destroy their own (as well as
> other) societies?
> They are largely from the middle and upper middle classes,
> often young (in their twenties), usually well educated, totally

5. Goodness knows where they got that name. Certainly they were not
symbiotic with respect to anything else. Could it be that they thought
"Symbionese" sounded vaguely like some native African group?

6. Robert F. Delaney, *A Study Guide for Terrorism,* Athens: Ohio University Press, 1980. Captain Robert F. Delaney, USNR (Ret), was Milton
Miles Professor of International Relations at the U.S. Naval War College,
1975–80.

dedicated, opinionated, dangerous, well trained, and invariably well armed.[7]

To add to Delaney's profile, it is worth nothing that most terrorists have a highly developed instinct for the jugular, a quality that separates the excellent from the run-of-the-mill strategists.

The best definition of the aim of terrorism that I have found also comes from that same study guide: ". . . the capture and control of the processes of social change."[8] Delaney goes on to note: "that not one military word is used in this definition [is] . . . significant because it establishes the distinction between a conventional military approach and the revolutionary approach of an insurgent enemy."

Terrorism is thus not basically a problem for the strategist of conventional armed forces, although specially trained units of the military services may be called on in situations where their unique expertise can be of particular use. Terrorism is inherently a problem for the police and for society and its civil leaders.

It is of interest to note, though, that the strategies of the terrorists do follow quite closely the general theory of strategy postulated in this book.

In their war against society, their aim is *"some selected degree of control* [of the processes of social change] *for . . .* [their] *own purpose."*[9] They seek to achieve this *"by control of the pattern"* of their war against society. And they do this by creating and manipulating a *"center of gravity"* (a person or an installation that will ensure public attention) which they have selected *"to the advantage of the strategist and the*

7. *Ibid.,* p. 23.

8. *Ibid.,* p. 58.

9. Italics indicate quotations from the preceding restated paragraphs of my general theory of strategy.

disadvantage of the opponent," the opponent being the organized society over which they want to exercise control.

Their pattern of operation is to control "*the nature and the placement and the timing and the weight of the centers of gravity*" that they have chosen "*toward* [their] *own ends*"— the control of the processes of social change. They select their targets for the greatest impact on that society.

Viewed in this context, the murder of Lord Mountbatten[10] and the often indiscriminate bombings in Belfast make a weird and repugnant sort of sense. So do the kidnappings in Beirut, the murder of Aldo Moro, the aborted piracy of the *Achille Lauro,* and the threats or the facts of bombing this or that public (and usually governmental) building.

Though I am sure none of them ever saw this small book, they do follow quite closely the theoretical model of strategy. And it is in part for this reason, to illustrate the validity of theory, that I have digressed to include terrorism in this postscript.

While it is not principally our problem in the armed forces, we do have at least two tasks growing directly out of the current spate of terrorism. One is to be on guard lest some element of our military forces, a ship or an air base or an arms cache, be converted into a center of gravity for manipulation and exploitation by terrorists. A second is to keep ready our specially trained units, always prepared to respond if our civil leaders and police need our support.

Terrorism is not going to disappear tomorrow.

Now let us take up another subject in this postscript.

There is one contemporary problem that almost cries out for comment. Twenty years ago, while discussing in Chapter

---

10. On 27 August 1979, the I.R.A. killed Mountbatten and other members of his family by a bomb placed on board his boat at Maullaghmore, Ireland.

5 the three generally recognized specific theories of strategy, the land, the sea, and the air, I added a fourth, the Mao theory, the "war of national liberation." This is the theory put to successful practice by Mao Tse-Tung, Vo Nguyen Giap, and Fidel Castro's theoretician, Che Guevara.

When I wrote of this, the United States was only then beginning its involvement in Viet Nam, and only within the past decade was the Somoza government in Nicaragua overthrown. Its successor government, the Sandinistas, was soon captured from within by the communists under the control and tutelage of Cuba and the Soviet Union.

In 1987 the United States was in a turmoil as to whether and how the Sandinista revolution could be recaptured and the communists, particularly the Soviets and the Cubans, could be ousted from control in Nicaragua.

Recall, if you will, that the Mao-Giap-Guevara theory is a system of measures by which a rural peasant society can defeat and replace an orthodox, essentially urban, government largely dependent on modern and relatively mechanized forces for its defense.

For the first time, the United States was in a position not to fight against a Mao-Giap-Guevara type of warfare, but to help a rural peasant society exploit this idea. The communists in Nicaragua were the existing, mainly urban, mechanized force. The original revolutionaries, having left or been forced out of the communist government, were part of the rural peasant base in which this new fourth specific theory of strategy would fit like a glove.

With all the to-do about whether and what to send to Nicaragua, it seemed to me that the first and most important items should have been thousands of copies of Che Guevara's writings on how to lay on a rural peasant revolt, minimally edited to make it ideologically democratic or even neutral rather than communist. With these ideas as a basis, the arms and food and medical supplies and all the other things would have a clearly focused purpose in the minds and actions of the rural peasant recipients.

Ironically, this application of an originally communist theory to our own use might just have turned the trick.

There have been, so far, four parts to this postscript to a book written a generation ago. The first part discussed strategic theory, the second part brought up to date a couple of the original strategic conclusions, the third part noted the application of strategic theory to the unlikely subject of terrorism, and the fourth part applied theory to a Central American problem.

I shall close by taking note of what could well be described as an emerging revolution in contemporary strategic thought, a revolution linked to changing technology.

The situation in the early nineteen-eighties was this:[11] For two or three decades the United States and Soviet Union had been in a race to see which could build the most devastating arsenal of nuclear weapons. Thus emerged the strategic concept of "mutual assured destruction," MAD, a peculiarly appropriate acronym. Toward the end of this period the Soviet Union had gradually drawn ahead, acquiring more powerful missiles with "multiple independent reentry vehicles," the MIRVs.

The response of the United States to this was a new missile, the MX, and with this new missile came a new exacerbation of the political strategic problems. Where do we put it? One proposal was a "racetrack" of many well-separated shelters to be built in the wide-open western states, with the mis-

---

11. The following sequence of events, which precedes my own comments, is adapted and condensed, perhaps too much to get the full flavor of this remarkable episode, from a thoroughly documented chapter of a book by Professor Frederick H. Hartmann, *Naval Renaissance: The U.S. Navy, 1980–1987* (Annapolis: Naval Institute Press, 1990).

siles themselves protected by being shuttled from one housing to another at random and in secrecy. The residents of these western states understandably protested at being made an area-wide target. An alternative proposal was that the MX missiles would be based close together in heavily fortified launch sites. And there were many objections to this "dense pack" proposal.

Pending the resolution of the "MX basing" problem, it was agreed more or less by default that the MX would be based in the existing silos of the older missiles.

Under the strategic concept of MAD, the citizens were becoming uncomfortable and restless with a growing frustration at dependence on the prospect of annihilation as our best defense. Along with this there was a persistent undercurrent of moral repugnance over the whole nuclear fission situation (which spilled over into protests against all forms of nuclear energy, including nuclear power plants).

During the same years that the nuclear weapons dilemma had been evolving, the electronic information-management revolution had been almost explosively expanding into its third generation. The first generation had been a product of electronic vacuum tubes. The second generation was "miniaturization," the replacement of vacuum tubes by transistors, which had, among other feats, made possible the distant early warning system of the 1950s and the earlier forays into space. And the third generation was the advent of "chips" that could "think" about anything the chip designers had built into them. This brought forth the encompassing computer revolution in the management and use of information. And this, in turn, has brought within reach the remote control and use of an almost incredible variety of vehicles in space.

Against this background, the Joint Chiefs of Staff held a series of meetings groping for resolutions, not only to the MX basing, but more importantly to the underlying dilemma of which MX basing was a symptom. Elsewhere in government, too, there were comparable disquieted gropings. The President, for instance, had appointed two committees to examine the matter.

In this climate of growing national uneasiness and frustration, Admiral James Watkins became the Chief of Naval Operations (and thus a member of the Joint Chiefs) in 1982. Himself a technically competent man, he set a small group of his own staff to examine some of the wider aspects of the problem. And then came a most fruitful luncheon meeting in which Dr. Edward Teller was Admiral Watkins's guest.

Dr. Teller spoke of his interest in project Excalibur, in which a small controlled nuclear reaction in a space vehicle would provide power for directed-energy weapons (X-ray lasers were among those mentioned) that could destroy or incapacitate missiles during their transit of space. Admiral Watkins recognized that the prevailing tenor of opinion in the United States probably would not accept even a controlled nuclear energy source in space, so he asked Dr. Teller whether the directed-energy weapons might be feasible with some other power source. And thus the conversation began to expand and to speculate on a wide variety of technological possibilities not yet in hand.

The result was an increase in the tempo of the intense and far-ranging examination, by Admiral Watkins and a small staff, of nonnuclear developments just over the technological horizon. The judgment was made that some would prove to be feasible and attainable, and Admiral Watkins proposed to the Joint Chiefs that they should adopt a policy to develop and test these more promising possibilities toward defense in space. The Joint Chiefs agreed and, with the chairman as their spokesman, took it to the President.

The result was the President's public proposal of the Strategic Defense Initiative, the SDI. The key words in his speech

110

were lifted without change from Watkins's and the Joint Chiefs' briefing paper: "*Protect* the American people, not just *avenge* them."

What had happened was this. The U.S. strategists had finally faced up to the fact that, in the intercontinental nuclear missile contest, they were confronted with a strategic dead end. No one could win, and not only the United States and the U.S.S.R. but the whole world might very well lose. Completely.

Then there came on the scene the possibility of defense, not previously considered technologically attainable, and this possibility raised other prospects. It could introduce the prospect of doubt into whatever might have been the attractiveness of a "first strike" by either side. It raised the admittedly distant prospect of eventually getting rid of vast numbers of nuclear weapons. It raised, even in the near term, an improved prospect of arms limitations agreements. And, most importantly, it shifted the conceptual initiative from the MAD concept of more and bigger weapons to defense against those weapons.

Let me restate that last paragraph in terms of abstract theory, in terms that will not have been used by the participants. The United States had been facing a strategic dead end: no way to win, no way to control military power. So it sought and found a new strategic "center of gravity." By introduction and development of this new conceptual center of gravity, the prospect of defense against intercontinental missiles as an alternative to MAD, they could regain a measure of control of the pattern (or the threat) of war, in this case to the advantage not only of the United States but of the entire world.[12] This radical departure from the prevailing conven-

_____

12. There were, of course, many other threads leading up to the SDI announcement by the President. To get a full appreciation of these, one must read Professor Hartmann's detailed recital of them. All I have done is

tional wisdom was bound to raise a storm of debate and protest from many quarters. Those wedded to the MAD concept
assured listeners that the new idea of SDI would not work: "It
is not possible." Those fearing diversion of funds from other
programs declared the SDI to be fiscal madness: "Waste bil-
lions of dollars." And many who had not been consulted in
the closely held development of the SDI proposals were almost automatic in their various "NIH" objections because (although no one said it out loud) it was "Not Invented Here."

The SDI proposal faced formidable opposition from the
start. But when looking ahead to its future, it is relevant to
recall two sentences from page 13 in the first chapter of this
book: "None of the really important aspects of strategy is out
of the public attention," and "The Congressman voting on a
military appropriation is, in a very real sense indeed, making
a fundamental strategic decision. . . ."

Let us hope, then, that our Congress does recognize this
rare opportunity to make a fundamental strategic decision—
whether or not to take control of this new center of gravity of
the world's nuclear strategy, the concept of defense in space,
and exploit it in a move toward a revolution in strategic thinking that could diminish or possibly replace the appalling and
repugnant concept of mutual assured destruction. The Congress and the people for whom it speaks are now in position
to make the most important strategic decision since the first
atomic explosion at White Sands.

There is more to this SDI concept, though, than its theoretical strategic validity, a strategic leverage with which to
climb out of the MAD morass. The idea of the SDI proposal is

___

to focus on the two related central facts: that the SDI concept of defense
against missiles was a revolutionary strategic idea; and that this concept of
defense, as contrasted to MAD, created a new strategic "center of gravity"
which can markedly redirect and alter strategic thought and the strategic
outlook from this time forward.

a vast national venture with a scientific and technological center of gravity.

Let me explain. Let me start with the premise, rather more frequently seen in print than we would like, that the United States is losing its worldwide leadership in many of the physical sciences and technological areas. This may well be true; and I think there is a reason for it, which I shall come to in a moment.

In the 1940s, the United States put its resources and its trust into a huge national venture, the quest for an atomic bomb. But we also got a great deal more than a bomb. We ended up with an enormous scientific and technological fallout, great numbers of unplanned, unexpected, and incalculably valuable byproducts of the Manhattan project. The most obvious were nuclear power plants, but there have also been advances in chemistry, in medicine, in laboratory physics, and in the macrophysics of the universe we live in.

In the 1950s we embarked on another, though less embracing, project, the Distant Early Warning or DEW Line. In the manned bomber days, this was the defense warning network reaching from Greenland and Alaska back to the North American Air Defense headquarters in a mountain in Colorado. This great radar and communications network would not have been possible with the bulky and temperamental electronic vacuum tubes. The first computer, built during World War II, was fitted with vacuum tubes and took up, literally, entire rooms with its bulk. At that rate, the computer revolution would never have gotten started. So someone invented the transistor in order to bring the equipment to manageable size. The unforeseen and serendipitous fallout from the electronic miniaturization of the DEW Line equipment was the start of the computer revolution. There were other byproducts, some of them conceptual, some of them in hardware, and probably most of them unrecognized as to their source, such as so simple a matter as worldwide telephone dialing. As a national venture, the DEW Line paid for itself a hundred times over.

In the 1960s, the United States put its energies into the space program and put men on the moon. And once again, the unforeseen collateral advances and benefits are beyond listing. They range from satellites for communication, for navigation, and for surveillance. And at the unglamorous end of the spectrum of unexpected results from the space program are baking dishes we can take out of the freezer and put straight into the oven without them cracking. The ceramic science of the nose cone gave us these dishes in the kitchen.

From these three great national ventures in the forties, the fifties, and the sixties, the United States reaped an unforeseen lush harvest of progress, the world's scientific and technological leadership.

In the 1970s the United States passed up a chance to venture into supersonic air travel. The French and the British combined, in a very tightly focused effort, to produce the Concorde. It may have been that this chance we passed up would not have been worth the gamble. I still have a lingering hunch that we should have gotten into that quest, but we will never know what the byproducts might have been from a full effort. We seem to be on the verge of missing another chance with SDI.

We have not had a wholehearted national venture into the scientific and technological unknown since the 1960s. I think this lapse in the sequence of these great national ventures is the reason we are beginning to slip back into the crowd. We are losing our leadership. So I do believe that there is a reason, complementary to the compelling strategic need, to embark on a fourth bold national effort in pursuit of the SDI goal. The chances look good that we could develop such a defense and escape the strategic dead end of MAD. And the chances look at least as good that out of such a national bold venture we could uncover conceptual and practical byproducts not even dreamt of here at the start. In such a mustering of national talents and national resources lies our hope of regained and reenergized scientific and national leadership.

In conclusion, as I look back upon my effort to devise a general theory of strategy, valid anytime, anyplace, and under any circumstance, I can see that time and technology have had an impact on my thinking. But on reflection, I think it is more an issue of how changing circumstances lead one to alter the emphasis when applying general theory to a particular situation rather than any fundamental change in theory. We still need to improve our vocabulary as we discuss strategy. The correlation between destruction and control is an issue in a major war as well as in recent cases of terrorism. The Central American issues of the 1980s involve consideration of changing our emphasis by using, rather than reacting to, the Mao theory. The question of SDI involves using new technology as leverage for control. And finally, our general experience over the past twenty years with technology, with terrorism, and with the whole range of questions under the heading of military strategy reemphasizes the profound interrelationship of strategy and the broad trends in national society.

APPENDIX A

Excerpt from "Reflections on the War in the Pacific" [1]

THERE ARE MANY ways to dissect a war in analyzing its strategy. It can be broken into Army, Navy, and Air Force; or it can be divided into defensive, defensive-offensive, and offensive; or it can be cut into military and non-military; or it can be divided in terms of time. But there is another way one can slice up a war for purposes of analysis: it can be done in terms of the general operational patterns of the strategies.

In doing this we shall discuss two operationally different kinds of strategies and we must employ descriptive adjectives not normally used in strategic matters. The classifications will be "sequential" and "cumulative" strategies.

Normally we consider a war as a series of discrete steps or actions, with each one of this series of actions growing naturally out of, and dependent upon, the one which preceded it. The total pattern of all the discrete or separate actions makes up, serially, the entire sequence of the war. If at any stage of the war one of these actions had happened differently, then the remainder of the sequence would have had a different pattern. The sequence would have been interrupted and altered.

The two great drives across the Pacific, MacArthur's campaign in the Southwest Pacific and the Central Pacific drive

---

1. This essay was originally published in the U.S. Naval Institute *Proceedings*, vol. 78, no. 4 (April 1952), pp. 351–361.

from Hawaii to the coast of China, can be analyzed as sequential strategies. Each one of these was composed of a series of discrete steps and each step could clearly be seen ahead of time, could clearly be appraised in terms of its expected result, and the result in turn would lead to the next step, the next position to be taken or the next action to be planned. This is what is meant by reference to a sequential strategy.

But there is another way to prosecute a war. There is a type of warfare in which the entire pattern is made up of a collection of lesser actions, but these lesser or individual actions are not sequentially interdependent. Each individual one is no more than a single statistic, an isolated plus or a minus, in arriving at the final result.

Psychological warfare might be such a matter, for instance, or economic warfare. No one action is completely dependent on the one which preceded it. The thing that counts is the cumulative effect. As a military example of this cumulative strategy the submarine campaign in the Pacific is superb.

The tonnage war waged by the American submarines in the Pacific is quite unlike the serial, the sequential, type of strategy. In a tonnage war it is not possible to forecast, with any degree of accuracy, the result of any specific action.

Any such war as these tonnage wars is an accumulation of more or less random individual victories. Any single submarine action is only one independent element in the cumulative effect of the total campaign.

So that in the Pacific, from 1941 to 1945, actually we conducted two separate wars against Japan. We conducted the sequential strategy campaigns, our drives across the Pacific to the coast of Asia and up to the shores of the Empire. And apparently quite apart from that we conducted a cumulative strategy aimed at Japan's economy. Oddly enough, these two went along together in time but essentially independently in their day-to-day activity.

We were able, with some degree of success, to predict in advance the outcome of the sequential strategy. We were not able, or at least we did not take advantage of whatever ability we had, to predict the result of the cumulative strategy. Somewhere along in 1944 we brought Japan, in large measure by pressure of this cumulative strategy, to a condition in which she had only two alternatives: to give in, or to approach national suicide. We are not, even today, able to tell precisely when that took place. But it did take place. Japan started the war with about six million tons of merchant shipping. During the early years of the war she acquired almost four million more. And by late 1944 nearly nine of this total of ten million tons had been destroyed. Japan had long since passed her point of no return. But we seemed not to know it, and possibly the Japanese did not know it.

The point to be made is this: there are actually two very different kinds of strategies to be used in war. One is the sequential, the series of visible, discrete steps, each dependent on the one that preceded it. The other is the cumulative, the less perceptible minute accumulation of little items piling one on top of the other until at some unknown point the mass of accumulated actions may be large enough to be critical. They are not incompatible strategies, they are not mutually exclusive. Quite the opposite. They are usually interdependent in their strategic result.

The sequential strategies all of us probably understand; the cumulative strategies possibly we do not. The latter, the cumulative, has long been a characteristic of war at sea. But there has been no conscious analytical differentiation of this cumulative warfare from the sequential in any of the major writings on strategy; and there is no major instance in which a cumulative strategy, operating by itself, has been successful. The French, for instance, were long addicted to their *guerre de course* at sea, but they never had it pay off in decisive victory by itself. The Germans have twice concentrated all their maritime effort on a cumulative strategy and have twice seen it fail.

But when these cumulative strategies have been used in conjunction with a sequential strategy, directed at the main object of the war, there are many instances in which the strength of the cumulative strategy has meant the difference between success or failure of the sequential. History abounds with examples in which a comparatively weak sequential strategy was enabled to reach victory by virtue of the strength of the cumulative strategy behind it. The Yorktown Campaign, the Peninsula Campaign in Portugal, or our own War between the States are three that come to mind. The First World War is another example. In this last war we seem not to have appreciated the strength of our cumulative strategy against Japan, operating as it did in support of the direct thrust to the critical goal.

Recognition of these two basically different kinds of strategy presents a new challenge to us, a challenge that could be a vitally important one. Our strategic success in the future may be measured by the skill with which we are able to balance our sequential and our cumulative efforts toward the most effective and least costly attainment of our goals. If we could judge the progress and the effect of our cumulative strategy, not only would we control an important element of strategy which up until now we have been forced to leave to chance, but we might more effectively shape the conditions existing when the war is over.

So, two specific suggestions: we should recognize the existence and the power of these cumulative strategies and integrate them more carefully into our basic plans; and we should study them more closely than we have done in order that we may be able to determine whether or not they profitably could be critical, and if they could, then to identify the points in their development at which they do become critical determinants in the progress of the war. When we do that we will be able to use them more efficiently and economically than we have in the past.

APPENDIX B

"On Maritime Strategy" [1]

O VER THE LAST half century there have been two generally accepted approaches to the study of maritime strategy. The first has been an analysis of the component elements of maritime strength, with Mahan's classification of these as geography, naval power, merchant marine, and the like usually serving as the basis for this kind of study. The second approach, more prevalent in our generation, is the discussion of strategy in terms of specific types of operations such as fast carrier strikes, anti-submarine warfare, or organized overseas transport. I think both of these avenues of approach tend to obscure, to some extent, the coherent form of the basic strategy that lies between these two, the strategy that grows from the components to give continuity and direction to the operations. It is this middle ground that I shall explore, the area in which a basic element of strength is transformed by an idea into a positive action. It is a sailor's concept of strategy, what it is, how it works, to what end it is followed, and what its problems are.

In doing this I shall present the subject from those four aspects that seem to me necessary for an adequately rounded appreciation both of the underlying idea and of the transla-

1. This essay was originally published in the U.S. Naval Institute *Proceedings,* vol. 79, no. 5 (May 1953), pp. 467–477.

tion of that idea into practical and useful results. These four aspects are, first, a theory of maritime strategy; second, past experience in the use of maritime strategy; third, some of the factors that complicate its use in our time; and fourth, our contemporary use of military power and the tendencies with respect to maritime strategy.

I. A THEORY OF MARITIME STRATEGY

The aim of any war is to establish some measure of control over the enemy. The pattern of action by which this control is sought is the strategy of the war. There are many types and levels of strategies, and many ways in which they may be classified. But since the subject of this discussion is maritime strategy, the classifications we shall use have already been determined. The three main streams of strategic thought in this sense are maritime strategy, continental strategy, and, more recently on the scene, air strategy.

Here, at the beginning of this discussion, it should be emphasized that clear-cut separations are artificial. In practice there is, and must be, a good deal of overlap and merging; the strategies are deliberately set apart from each other in this treatment of the subject only for purposes of study and analysis.

I use the term continental strategy to indicate a pattern of employment of armed forces in which the major and critical part of the action to establish control over the enemy is directed against his armies along a central land axis. All other efforts are in support of the central drive of this continental strategy. In spite of the descriptive title that I have elected to use for this type of strategy, the involvement of an entire continent is not necessarily implied.

The term air strategy I use to indicate an over-all war strategy in which the decision is sought primarily by air action, with predominant emphasis on strategic bombardment. All other efforts are to a greater or lesser degree subordinate to that.

A maritime strategy is one in which the world's maritime communications systems are exploited as the main avenues by way of which strength may be applied to establish control over one's enemies.

Maritime strategy normally consists of two major phases. The first, and it must be first, is the establishment of control of the sea. After an adequate control of the sea is gained comes the second phase, the exploitation of that control by projection of power into one or more selected critical areas of decision on the land.

Too often the first or blue-water phase of maritime strategy is regarded as the whole process rather than no more than the necessary first half. Most naval history, for example, concerns itself with the struggles for control of the sea, the naval battles, the protection of commerce, and the blockade in one form or another.

This phase, also, is the one that attracts the greater part of our own professional attention, and it is the phase that most landsmen accept as the entire concept when one introduces the subject of maritime strategy.

Within the first phase, the control-of-the-sea segment of the over-all pattern, there are initially two components of control. They will be considered separately for analytic purposes, although the actual conduct in war may so closely interweave them that the separate goals may not be superficially apparent. One of these components is ensuring one's own use of the sea; the other is denial to the enemy of his use of the sea. At least in the early stages of the struggle for control, these two goals can be analytically considered more or less apart from each other; and, as long as neither contestant predominates in both, there remains a fairly clear delineation of these two functional components of the struggle for control. Not until one sea power emerges as dominant in both these components do the two of them merge into the single problem of positive and wilful control of all that moves at sea. This is the ideal condition that has many times been striven for but never, except possibly at the very end of the War in the Pacific, been attained in near perfection.

The naval strategies (as differentiated from the more inclusive maritime strategies) and the naval tactics of both contestants are largely determined by the status and progress of the struggle for control.

If, for instance, two nations having roughly equal naval strength go to war, the attention of each of them must be devoted primarily to the fight for naval supremacy. This type of naval contest has a dual purpose in that it embraces both components of control of the sea—the positive aim of securing one's own use of the sea (by destroying the force that could hazard that use), and the negative aim of denying to the enemy his use of the sea (destroying the force that could protect him). This was the case in the recent War in the Pacific when the American and Japanese fleets fought it out until we finally established an ocean-wide control adequate to our needs.

A somewhat different situation exists when two opposing nations start with unequal naval strength. The primary aim of the stronger in this situation is to protect and extend its own use of maritime communications by both passive and active means—passive in defending its own forces at sea, and active in seeking out and destroying enemy forces that offer threat to the use of the sea by the stronger power. The primary aim of the weaker is to interfere with the stronger's use of the sea by resort to some specialized technique, such as a war of attrition, a deliberate hoarding of naval threat, or an attack on the stronger's commerce. This was the case in the last two wars in the Atlantic when Germany, as the weaker, hoarded her major combatant ships and placed her hopes in her attacks on allied commerce.

126

There are many refinements to be applied to this theoretical outline in the actual struggle for control of the sea. Particularly in the early part of a war, control is normally in dispute with neither antagonist able to utilize the sea to his own satisfaction. This dispute leads to two other situations which are frequently encountered; one is local control of some part of the sea, and the other is temporary control. The two are frequently combined as when the Germans attained a temporary local control of the waters off Norway long enough to permit their invasion and consolidation of that position. The control of the Mediterranean was in dispute for the first three years of the recent war, with both sides at times having temporary control of the Central Mediterranean, while the British, except for one indecisive moment, never lost local control at either end.

This is an all too brief outline of the problem of control of the sea, the necessary first phase of a maritime strategy. When a maritime power is reasonably successful in securing the sea to its own use (that is, in repressing the enemy's power to interfere unduly), then it can turn to the second, or exploitation, phase of maritime strategy. And here the subject becomes considerably more slippery, which is really not surprising since it is, in actual fact, a far more subtle proposition than most of us initially realize.

In order to discuss the exploitation of sea power it is necessary to return to the premise that opened this discussion, the assertion that "the aim of any war is to establish some measure of control over the enemy." If this premise is accepted (and its acceptance in general substance is critical to this theory of warfare), then the next step is the examination of methods of establishing control.

In wars between powers having their major strength in ground forces, the defeat of one of the two contending armies has generally led to victory. This has been the situation when

127

two continental strategies have opposed each other. In wars in which at least one of the two contestants was a major sea power, the defeat of one contending navy and the establishment by the other of control of the sea has generally led to victory. But this victory has been reached only when the dominant sea power has exploited his strength at sea by projecting at least one other element of force to establish control over the enemy on the land.

In some cases the strength at sea has enabled the naval victor to launch a ground force into a critical part of the other's territory. In these instances the soldiery has been the direct instrument of control that clinched the issue at hand. The seaborne invasions of Sicily and Italy a decade ago were the exploitation by ground forces of the naval seizure of control of the sea. We have already noted the sea-and-air-borne invasion of Norway by the Germans. This was an exploitation, using ground forces, by a nation with temporary control of the local sea area.

Another means of exploitation by sea power is the use of economic force for the application of control. When the Armada was defeated, England intensified her blockage of Spanish trade with the New World and eventually choked Spain almost to death. Spain has never recovered. In the Anglo-Dutch Wars, England established her naval control at sea and was in position to clamp down on Dutch commerce as she had done against the Spanish. But the Dutch saw what was in prospect, acknowledged the potential strength of British control (augmented by Britain's geographic advantage), and reached agreement with Britain before having to undergo the painful process of having all Dutch commerce destroyed. In the case of the recent war with Japan, the advancing American control of the sea was exploited to stifle Japanese overseas communications. Economic suffocation was the primary instrument that enforced Japanese acquiescence. She was dependent on sea communications, not only for her existence as a major power, but for her very life.

There are a few instances in which the instrument of control has been some other force, a political pressure of this-for-that, a direct or indirect bribery of men having power decision, or a revolt somewhere inside the structure of the enemy power. But the main methods by which force has been applied to establish control over the enemy have been these three: a victory by the armies of one land power over another; a victory by a sea power exploiting her power at sea to project a frequently smaller but strategically decisive ground force for the actual establishment of control on land; and a victory by a sea power exploiting her power at sea to project an economic force toward the eventual establishment of governing control over the enemy in his own land. It is the second and third of these, the two main methods of exploiting power at sea, that form the basis of the second phase of maritime strategy.

It should be noted that, in practice, the exploitation of sea power is usually a combination of general slow stiflings with a few critical thrusts. These latter are frequently spectacular and draw our attention to the exclusion of the former, while in point of fact the critical thrusts would not be critical were it not for the tedious and constant tightening of the screws that makes them possible.

II. AN ILLUSTRATION OF MARITIME
STRATEGY IN USE

Up to this point I have outlined the basic pattern of action from which a maritime strategy may be compounded, never in pure form, of course, but with the appropriate blending of armies and navies and air forces, and of political and economic and psychological forces.

Now, after this theoretic description of maritime strategy, let us examine a specific problem. How might we evolve a strategy for the United States and how would we judge its validity today?

I think the soundest way to reach toward answers in any such inquiry is first to turn to comparable historical experience, to recognize the points both of similarity and of difference in the two situations, and then to take advantage of that experience in light of our own specific circumstances.

The recent war with Japan is already accepted as the modern naval classic. But the problems faced in a war with insular Japan and the problems faced in a possible war with a continental great power are not the same. I do not think the War in the Pacific is a valid precedent to turn to for a study of maritime strategy relevant to a war with a power whose base is Eurasia. Correspondingly, I do believe that much of the confusion in our present naval thinking is the result of trying, without careful discrimination, to adapt the war with Japan to a prospective war with a great land power.

Let us look at our situation. We are a great sea power, geographically set apart from the continent by intervening waters. Our hypothetical opponent, a great land power with a much smaller sea power potential, is firmly in control of much of Europe and is seriously threatening the rest. Has that situation ever existed before? And how was it managed?

Yes, that situation has existed before, several times, under reasonably similar circumstances. It existed and was managed with a fair degree of similarity in the First World War and again in the Second World War. But it was managed in what I think was an even closer analogy a hundred and fifty years ago. I have selected that third one as our point of departure in this discussion because it illustrates the application of a maritime strategy with fewer obscuring complexities than either of the two more recent situations. I shall outline the experience of Britain in defeating Napoleon and then, after the skeleton of that strategic process is exposed to view, superimpose on it some of the complicating factors that confront the strategist today.

The British struggle with Napoleon illustrates quite clearly the two major phases of maritime strategy. At the start of the war, late in the eighteenth century, both Britain and France had a major strength at sea. The struggle initially was a struggle between fleets for control of the sea, a control that was in dispute for many years. This is the portion of maritime history that most of us are familiar with, and this is the first phase that was completed with the successful campaign culminating in the victory at Trafalgar.

The second phase of that great war is remarkably unappreciated. It opened with Britain's having gained control of the sea at Trafalgar, and it is here that I am going to draw the comparison with our situation today. We have the potential, if not the actual strength, to establish a workable control of the sea. It need scarcely be said that this will take considerable doing, but I do not question that we can gain control of the sea when we need it.

So let us start from that point in 1805, well along in the middle of the war. At that time Britain, as a major sea power, found herself facing the problem of how to defeat France, a major land power, firmly in control of much of Europe and threatening the rest.

The ten years from Trafalgar to the final downfall of Napoleon in 1815 present, at first glance, a very confusing picture. Over all the scene lay the shadow of the seemingly irresistible and enduring strength of the Emperor's armies. There was a succession of apparently disconnected battles from one end of Europe to the other. There was a continuing bitter economic warfare that reached its climax with the Berlin and Milan Decrees by which Napoleon tried to exclude Britain from her markets. These were met with the Orders in Council by which Britain attempted to control and limit the commerce of Europe to her own advantage. There were unsteady and changing governments, now opposed and now subordinate to Napoleon. There was propaganda, intrigue, bribery, and treachery. And all through that period there were the tremendous British grants of monies to potential allies all over Europe; indeed, Britain literally financed most of Europe at one time or another during those turbulent ten years of war. When examined in terms of these details, it seems almost incredible that Britain ever won. But when the entire period is taken under scrutiny, then three fundamental factors, superimposed on the basic and continued maintenance of her control of the sea, emerge to give coherence to the actions over those years.

First, Britain, in the exploitation of her maritime strength, never slackened her pressure on the French all around the periphery of the Empire. The economic war was waged bitterly and continuously, and advantage was taken of every economic strain that developed within the continental system.

Second, Britain, in exploitation of her sea communications, never missed an opportunity to launch an army against a vulnerable point in Napoleon's armed strength. Whenever the Emperor moved one way, then Britain and whoever happened to be her allies at the moment stabbed from the other. In Portugal, in Spain, in Austria, in the Low Countries, in the Baltic, Napoleon was never secure. Whenever Napoleon managed to counter these threats with his own greater force, then Britain took her profits, cut her losses, and withdrew, biding her time till opportunity showed again.

Illustrative of the pressures on Napoleon from the sea were the concurrent activities of two British commanders, the Duke of Wellington in the Iberian Peninsula and Admiral Sir James Saumarez in the Baltic. In 1811 while Wellesley was producing what Napoleon described as the "Spanish ulcer," Saumarez, commanding the dominant sea strength along northern Europe, brought about some unpublicized but critically important secret meetings on board his flagship. In these he induced agreements with Sweden and Russia in which the Czar was given the military and political freedom that he needed to turn on Napoleon. This soon brought Napoleon's armies from Spain into Russia, and that wholesale calamity in 1812 needs no comment except to note that it could never have happened had not British sea power been applied with remarkable political agility in Napoleon's rear.

Third, in the exploitation of her sea power Britain never did formulate and commit herself to a single military plan by which she expected to win the war. She never lost sight that her goal was the defeat of Napoleon; she never missed a chance to apply pressure where it hurt; but there was no constricting rigidity of plan nor any premature commitment in her strategy. Basic to her maritime concept was her practice of taking timely advantage of opportunity as it opened to her.

In our own contemporary atmosphere of intensive and inclusive planning, we might pause to realize anew this peculiar advantage in exploitation of sea power. It is the capacity to manipulate the placement, the timing, and, in great measure, the weight of the strategic centers of gravity on the land.

Britain had the ability and the will, and she exploited to the fullest her control of the maritime communications systems of the world. Operating from the base of her firm control at sea, Britain and her allies continued their penetration of every crevice in Napoleon's armor until finally his structure fell at his heels. Napoleon himself seems never to have realized that it was the ubiquity of Britain's sea power that lent the repeatedly resurgent and finally victorious strength in the defeating of Napoleon.

How truly remarkable is the similarity between today and a century and a half ago. The shadow of the dictator's army over the unwilling peoples of Europe. Their hope of independence to be regained with the help of the sea power from off the continent. The Berlin Decrees in the one case and the Iron Curtain in the other, and the intense efforts in both to build an independent economy behind these barriers. The pulling and hauling in the formation of alliances with the great maritime strength of the day. The struggling free nations of Europe helped to their feet by the financial and economic strength of the power across the sea. And the clear understanding by these two great maritime nations, then Great Britain and now the United States, that Europe must be kept free of dominance by a single power if they would themselves survive.

III. FACTORS THAT COMPLICATE
MODERN STRATEGIES

These are the similarities in the two situations today and a hundred and fifty years ago. But striking as they are we can not disregard the fact that intervening between that time and this are the tremendous upheavals of the industrial revolution, its contemporary successor the technological revolution, and the continuing social and political revolution that still surges throughout the world. These have changed the tools and techniques of warfare almost beyond recognition. In many important respects the visible and active appearance of warfare bears little or no resemblance to that of a century and a half ago. But more subtle than these obvious changes in combat activities are the problems of whether and how the modern innovations have altered the underlying patterns of war, the basic strategies of war. While many of the skills of men-of-warsmen today bear little relation to those of the men who sailed under Collingwood, can we properly infer that the strategic problems that faced Collingwood and Nelson and Barham and Pitt are equally unrelated to those facing their successors today? That question is the one at hand when we set ourselves to judge the value of yesterday's experience in today's situation.

In order to open up that question I have selected six major complications of warfare that have grown out of the industrial revolution to perplex the strategist today, six problems that either did not exist before or have undergone such marked change as to be in fact new problems. These are: mechanization in war, explosives in war, arms and revolution, logistics in war, the phenomenon of flight, and nuclear energy in war. This is certainly not an exhaustive list, but it is, I think, an indicative one. The extent to which these matters alter the fundamental pattern of action by which we seek to establish control in war is the extent to which we must modify yesterday's experience in applying it to today's situation.

MECHANIZATION IN WAR

When we consider the industrial revolution, we realize at once the unbelievable progress that has given us tanks and jeeps and steam vessels and submarines and automatic weapons. The difference between a primitive or man-power armed force and an industrial or mechanized armed force is apparent. But all the problems growing from these differences have not yet been generally recognized. Our military attention has been concentrated almost exclusively on the problem of fighting one mechanized armed force with another mechanized armed force. That is true in all three of the services, Army, Navy, and Air Force. However, there are two other problems to be considered. One is the business of devising strategies and tactics for use by relatively primitive armed forces against highly mechanized ones; the other, devising strategies and tactics for use by mechanized forces against primitive forces. That latter problem is a very real one. It faces us today in Korea, and I think we have failed to recognize it as basic. It is a direct challenge to the validity of the strategic concepts applied in Korea. It would be a challenge in a much greater field if the war were to widen.

Our present weapons and techniques are the best we can devise for use against armed forces such as our own. The question we must ask is: are our present strategic concepts, techniques, and weapons also the best that we can devise for use against armed forces whose primary strength is man-power rather than highly refined and complicated machine power?

With respect to ground forces the importance of this query may not be too critical as long as the infantry remains recognized as the focal point of ground strength. That should insure maintenance of the man-power perspective no matter how much machinery may be involved.

With respect to naval forces, a careful pondering of this question could, I believe, lead to a shift of emphasis in our fleet preparations from the blue-water reaches of the sea to the inshore soundings. Apart from countering the atypical (though very real) hazard of uniquely efficient submarines, I believe that a large proportion of our naval effort, particularly in the exploitation phase of a next war, must be put into tools and techniques that can seize and exploit control of the shoal and restricted waters along the enemy littoral and penetrating into the enemy territory. This subject deserves elaboration, but there has yet been no satisfactory statement of the problem, much less a satisfactory approach toward its solution. That a problem does exist, that it will require a fairly large change in prevailing strategic concepts, and that it will require the evolution of basically simple tools and techniques not now at hand, I am sure. But no one has yet been able to suggest the shape of a generally valid concept tailored to this need, nor the particular functions of the tools that we must adapt or devise. The problem concerns the maintenance and exploitation of control on inshore waters, a matter that I think was handled better a century and a half ago than it is today.

With respect to air forces, the problem takes a somewhat different turn. While there is no such thing as a primitive or man-power air force, we do find ourselves faced with the business of fighting a relatively primitive force with a highly mechanized air force. It is a problem that must be faced by naval aviation as well as by independent air forces. Here, more than anywhere else, we have fallen into the trap of casting the enemy in our own image. To use a specific illustration: we have done all our planning of air interdiction on the assumption that, if the interdicting effort is strong enough, it will succeed. Against highly mechanized ground forces this may well be true; such ground forces are a most susceptible target. Against a piggy-back army, one whose basic reliance is in men and animals, I think this assumption is not valid. The point is that the theory of interdiction, air against ground, must be modified to the extent that the possible effectiveness of interdiction is a function in part of the strength of the interdicting force and in equal part of the susceptibility of the target to interdiction. A highly mechanized target is maximally vulnerable; as the target becomes more primitive, the susceptibility approaches zero.

That is one type of modern complication that the strategist, maritime or otherwise, must consider.

EXPLOSIVES IN WAR

Now let us take up a different aspect of the industrial revolution. Gradually, over the last century, the function of explosives in warfare has changed, and I think we have missed the significance of this change.

Originally the explosives, gunpowder in one form or another, were used primarily as a propellant for missiles. The purpose of these missiles was direct destruction—the direct

137

killing men or the sinking of ships. This led to an efficient imposition of control with little or none of what I shall describe as "over-kill." This word I use to indicate that proportion of effort which cannot be used for the direct establishment of control.

Today the infantry rifle is the remnant of this once universal method of warfare. We now use explosives as a propellant as we did before. But we also use explosives both as an agent of destruction at the target and as the on-target propellant of secondary missiles of destruction. The nature of contemporary industrialized and mechanized targets, both civilian and military, invites the use of explosives against them on a grand scale. Modern methods encourage the use of explosives as a general agent of destruction.

A result of this has been a prevailing tendency to equate destruction with war, and this in turn leads us to associate the idea of maximum destruction with victory.

In this partly justified and partly superficial thinking, there is a fallacy. That fallacy is our forgetting that the purpose of destruction in war must be the achievement of control. Other than that it has no point. The degree to which destruction contributes to control is the degree to which it contributes to final victory. Destruction by the massive use of explosives carries with itself the inherent characteristic of a large proportion of over-kill (with its very important secondary effects) and thus a lessened proportion of direct control.

The relationship between destruction and control in war is one critical measure of the efficiency of the conduct of war.

The maritime strategist has long been aware of this, his appreciation emphasized by the comparative economy forced on him by the nature of the tools with which he works. The essence of the exploitation of sea power is the projection of concentrated power to critical points of decision, the establishment of a maximum of control with a minimum of war's general destruction. From this has grown the sailor's firm belief in the need of peculiarly specialized types of ground strength and of air strength as built-in components of maritime strength in order that he may impose his decisive control at critical points of his own choosing. This is a compelling reason why marines and aviators are integral units of the naval service.

ARMS AND REVOLUTION

In addition to mechanization in war and the role of explosives in war, there is a third facet of the industrial revolution in war that, in a different field, modifies somewhat the classic patterns of strategy.

During the Napoleonic Wars and until fairly recently, it has been possible for any determined people to revolt almost at will. Before mechanization it was a relatively simple matter for any dissident group to lay its hands on the necessary tools of war and revolution. Some pikes and halberds could be improvised; smooth-bores and even rifles could be made or stolen and stored locally until the time came for their use. But the tools of warfare have grown so complex and expensive within the last two generations that in a modern society only the state itself can organize and pay for the production of arms. This means that the support of an army, with its arms, is now a necessary ingredient of revolution. Unless a state's own army joins the rebels, then the help of an outside army must be directly available before any revolution can be successful.

This concerns air strategy to whatever extent airborne and air-supported troops may be adequate to the needs, though even this is more a matter of ground force than of air force interest. More fundamentally, it concerns continental and maritime strategy. An outright revolt within the enemy's political or military structure must not be encouraged until an adequate and sympathetic ground force is directly at hand to support it. This limits the possible areas of revolt in war to those along a continental front or along the accessible littoral behind the front. Since this restriction on revolution has developed, a mobile sea-borne and sea-supported ground force has become increasingly important to the exploitation of this type of potential weakness in an enemy.

LOGISTICS IN WAR

Directly related to the growth of the industrial and technological revolutions is the problem of modern logistic support. Primitive armies could, and to a large extent still can, live off the country. Mechanized armies can not. A fleet under sail could stay at sea almost indefinitely; indeed, Nelson kept his Toulon blockade for over two years without once leaving his flagship. A modern navy can stay at sea for considerable time, to be sure, but not without enormous effort in logistic support. Air forces, while there is no pre-industrial comparison, are by their nature the most logistically helpless element of armed force. In all types of strategies, continental, maritime, or air, the logistic factor must weigh heavily in arriving at decisions, both with respect to the quality and quantity of material needed and with respect to the time and cost required for its delivery.

It is of interest to compare the three basic types of strategies in the matter of logistic vulnerability. In the continental strategy, the mechanized army is far more vulnerable than its predecessor by reason of its logistic dependence. While it is tactically more mobile, it is strategically an infinitely more ponderous mass to move or to redirect. In a strategy basically maritime, the bulk and complexity of logistic support is incalculably greater than that of the classic sea powers, but the application of logistic support may actually be a good bit easier. Easier not only compared to primitive maritime force but compared to mechanized continental force. The flexibility of contemporary maritime communications systems compared to those on land, and the lesser degree to which they can be critically interrupted after control is established at sea, combine to make the exploitation phase of a maritime strategy quite attractive when balanced against a drive toward a similar goal by over-land avenues.

After indicating the scope of the industrial revolution's logistic effect on both continental and maritime strategies we can see that, while it is complicating, it is not unique. The problems involved are not novel; they are distorted and magnified, but they do not invalidate the traditionally accepted bases either of the continental or of the maritime strategies.

With respect to air strategy—and here I am going to merge logistics with the next major topic, that of flight—the logistic effect of the industrial revolution takes a somewhat different turn. The logistic problems introduced by the industrial revolution are the basis of prevailing air power theory. The theory of strategic bombardment and the theory of interdiction are both predicated on an assumption of critical vulnerability of the enemy's logistic support. In comparing the capacities of continental or maritime strategies with air strategy, or in the weighing of any derivative lesser strategies, the first point of examination should be this: to what degree is the assumption of the enemy's logistic vulnerability valid? The continental or maritime strategies are not completely dependent on this or on any other one assumption; the air strategy is. Only to the degree that this assumption of critical vulnerability is accepted can a comparison be continued past this initial point. Only to this degree can we then make inquiry as to the relation between logistic destruction and the achievement of strategic control. Only within these limits can judgments be valid.

FLIGHT

Quite apart from the logistic base of the specialized theory of air power, the phenomenon of flight has had three generally recognized effects on warfare.

First, it has extended the range and quality of observation in the conduct of war, enough so that both the tactics and the strategies of war have been affected. This change in the range and quality of observation has probably affected naval warfare more than war on the land. Flight has had more influence than any other factor on the management of the age-old problem of the unlocated enemy.

Second, flight has extended the range and affected the use of destruction in war and altered the comparative value of targets of destruction. The relative importance, for instance, of cities in warfare, now that they have become industrial centers of power, has undergone quite a change since the coming of the airplane.

Third, flight has introduced a new capacity for transportation, a capacity whose capabilities and limitations are so well understood that they need not be detailed here.

These three effects of flight—the changes in observation, destruction, and transportation in war—have not lacked for attention in military thought.

Finally, flight has introduced the proposition that there exists another great basis of strategic thought, that is, air power as distinguished from sea power and land power. Needless to say this proposition has not been universally accepted, and the skeletal frame of dispute with respect to air power theory has not yet been made clear. Until that is done, there can be no general acceptance or rejection of the theories of air strategy, and that lack of general acceptance or rejection is the point I wish to make. I believe a very real influence on strategic decision in any military or naval problem is created, not only by the obvious existence of flight, but by the uncertainty stemming from efforts to fit it into its proper and accepted place with corresponding military and naval activity. The maritime strategist must adapt his practices not only to the physical fact of flight but to the psychological fact of uncertainty as to its niche in the military power complex.

NUCLEAR ENERGY IN WAR

A direct result of the technological revolution is nuclear energy. We have already experienced its logarithmic increase in capacity for destruction. We are beginning to see a comparable increase in capacity for movement. We seem to be fairly well beyond the emotional shock associated with its initial display. And we are acquiring acceptably objective information as to the capabilities of nuclear weapons in terms of direct destructive effects.

It seems to me that the primary unsolved problem in the field of military employment of nuclear weapons is the problem of explosives and their over-kill—the relationship between destruction and control that has already been introduced into the discussion.

In tactical terms the results are probably calculable. Against military targets on the land or the sea, the effect of atomic bombs will be to force a revision of the pre-atomic techniques. Against non-military targets, the imponderables decidedly complicate the issues. I believe the availability in fair quantity of nuclear weapons will force us either to re-examine our notions as to what may be acceptable results of war, or to re-examine our apparent intentions with respect to their employment. This problem, of course, is closely related to the one we face in appraising the position of aviation in the total military power structure.

The maritime strategist, I think, is fortunate in that the nature of his strategic theory does not induce an almost inevitable dependence on the use of nuclear weapons against non-military targets. So much, in those cases, is beyond calculation. Success is dependent to a governing degree not on what

143

we do but on what the enemy does. We can not accurately predict enemy behavior, and thus we must gamble on how an enemy will react to the side effects of the considerable over-kill inherent in the use of nuclear weapons. That is a most difficult hurdle to overcome when one's goal is recognized not as the delivery of destruction but the establishment of control over the enemy.

IV. THE PATTERN OF STRATEGY TODAY

These six problems introduced into warfare within the last few generations are all of major importance. All of them, in one way or another, have appeared to "revolutionize" strategy. Certainly each of them has markedly altered the climate in which the strategist operates and has modified the techniques with which he puts his strategy to practice. But none of them, in my belief, has yet demonstrated conclusively that it has changed the basic patterns of strategy. These problems and others like them are still in the process of digestion in all phases of warfare. They are problems that can be resolved and, in most cases, are being resolved in practical application. The capacity of a maritime strategy to adapt itself to these major changes is one of the reasons why I believe a maritime strategy should be a most attractive one to the United States in her present situation. Let us see how it is working in practice today.

As early as 1946 the United States became aware that there was a very real possibility of all of Europe's falling under the domination of a single great power. There were different interpretations of the type of hazard that this situation would present—military, political, social, economic, or ideological hazard—but these need not concern us. We may start from the point where a hazard was recognized and trace our action from there.

144

Greece and Turkey were both under pressure by Soviet Russia. It was to the interest of the United States to prevent communist domination in those two countries. They were given military and economic assistance by the United States in sufficient strength to offset the communist pressure. This is most interesting because of the geographic situation involved. One of these countries has a land border common to Russia; the other, a land border common to a Russian satellite. Both of them are about five thousand miles from the United States. But both of them are accessible by sea. This situation gives rise to the astonishing paradox: Greece and Turkey are closer to the United States, in political and economic and military terms, than they are to Russia. The common frontier of the sea and our exploitation of maritime communications systems make these two countries more accessible to us than to the communists.

During the late 1940's several of the Central European nations tried to stay out, or break out, of the Russian orbit. Poland, Czechoslovakia, Rumania, Hungary, and Bulgaria succumbed. Only Jugoslavia succeeded in breaking out of the Iron Curtain. Of all these countries, only Jugoslavia had access to a sea under Western control. I think that fact is significant; and I also think that if we had had control of the Baltic we would not have lost Poland.

Later NATO was formed. Many men fail to realize that this North Atlantic Treaty Organization is, by its very name, an alliance of maritime nations. The common bond in NATO is the bond of the maritime communications system centered in the North Atlantic. It is significant that Turkey, at the far end of the Mediterranean, which we control, is a member of NATO, while Sweden, at the very entrance to the Baltic, which we do not control, is not a member of NATO.

In the early days of NATO, a military organization was started for the immediate purpose of insuring the survival of the Western nations on the Continent. The structure of this organization indicated that it was designed for immediate defense against the direct military hazard of the continental strategy opposed to it. Since that time the NATO organization has been filled out. The Supreme Allied Commander in Europe is properly an army commander. His Commander in Chief, North, is functionally and properly a naval commander. His Commander in Chief, South, should be for the same reason a naval commander. The Supreme Allied Commander, Atlantic, co-equal with the Supreme Allied Commander Europe, is, as he must be, a naval commander. This present organization means that the United States and her colleagues in alliance clearly recognize the value of a strategy whose governing element is control of the maritime communications systems.

Let us compare the implications of this command organization with the elements of a maritime strategy that we identified at the beginning of this discussion. The first phase would be to establish control of the sea. The Supreme Allied Commander Atlantic and the two subordinate naval commanders of SACEur, the CinCNorth and the CinCSouth, are organizationally situated to insure that control. The second phase would be the exploitation of sea power. The two commanders on the north and south of Europe not only command naval forces, but they command the needed associated ground and air forces to exploit the control of the sea that they establish. The Commander in Chief Atlantic is in position, not only to insure reliable communications and support for his opposite number on the continent, but also to apply the power of his maritime strength either directly to Western Europe or through the sea on either flank by way of the commanders-in-chief in the north and south. The Sixth Fleet, for instance, is basically an Atlantic unit potentially applied at present through the CinCSouth.

Vast though it be, this is only a portion of the total picture.

NATO does not include all of the United States' interests, nor does it include all of the British interests, in potential wars all around the globe. These two nations are additionally and individually organized outside of NATO, so that each of them may apply its own maritime strength in its own interests around the whole periphery of the Eurasian continent. There is difference in scale and difference in emphasis, but the underlying concepts are the same.

In this struggle between East and West, the Western nations are organizing toward the full exploitation of the flexibility, resilience, endurance, and concentrated application of power that can lead to decisive control when it is needed. The whole Western world is placing its faith in the concept of a strategy that is basically maritime.

APPENDIX C

"Why a Sailor Thinks
Like a Sailor"[1]

E VERY AUTUMN there is a series of internal crises in the
Navy Department, growing in intensity until finally the
annual budget requests take shape. During the winter the Department of Defense and the Congress work over the budgets
of all three services to try to get them into some kind of acceptable meshing. Then finally in the spring, before the Congress goes home for the summer, there is usually some sort of
an eruption into public debate related to authorizations or
appropriations or changes in laws governing the services.

A couple of years ago it was Reorganization Plan 6. Last
year it was the Symington Hearings. No one knows exactly
what the subject may be in the months just ahead—budget
allocations, or a common supply system, or efficiency, or
economy, or civilian control, or an earlier spring, or a combination of any or all of them.

The only thing we can be fairly sure of is that the services
will, somehow, find themselves in some sort of public opposition. And, whatever may be the point at issue, each of the services will have strong ideas and clear ones on its own side of
the discussion.

1. This article was originally published in the U.S. Naval Institute *Proceedings,* vol. 83, no. 8 (August 1957), pp. 811–817.

The basic problem is why they do not agree. Why does the soldier think like a soldier, the sailor like a sailor, and the airman like neither of these but like an airman?

Let there be no delusion. Even though they all serve the same common purpose and do so in all the honesty and sincerity of able and dedicated men, they do not think alike. There are areas of agreement and coincidence, to be sure, and these are by far the most numerous and inclusive. But there are areas of differences, important differences, even though they may be subtle and hard to isolate and hold up for examination.

Before going further, it would be well to inject a caution: Asking why they do not agree is quite a different matter from asserting that they should agree. On the contrary, these differences of judgment, these clashes of ideas, these almost constant pullings and haulings among the services, are the greatest source of military strength that the nation has. We do differ, within and among the services, and may Heaven help us if we ever enter into a period of prevailing sweetness and light and unanimity. Nothing would be more dangerous to our nation than the comfortable and placid acceptance of a single idea, a single and exclusively dominant military pattern of thought. The political parallel is almost too obvious to mention.

Let us only recognize that the unique advantage we have over the monolithic organizations which may oppose us is built into our system politically and militarily—the capacity to detect and expose our own weaknesses. As a concomitant of that we have always at hand an intellectual reserve, a reserve of strategic concept, the capacity to put to practice an alternate plan of action.

Strangely enough, the one aspect of the situation that has never really been publicly aired, nor even examined with enough perception and depth to make it worth the effort, is the underlying basis of the disagreement. Why *do* the soldiers think one way, and the sailors another, and the airmen still a third?

There will be no attempt in this discussion to speak for the soldier and the airman. The aim here will be to try to sketch out some foundations of the sailor's thought pattern—why he thinks the way he does. To do this, we shall take up a few war-planning assumptions, and then take up briefly the maritime concept of warfare. Then, after that, perhaps the package can be related to the general tasks of war and to one or two specific current problems to demonstrate the effect of these basic patterns of thought on the sailor's attitude toward the matters of the times.

As for the matter of war-planning assumptions, they are brought into this discussion for two reasons. First, because the planning phase of strategy is the link between the ideas of war and the conduct of war. And second, because recognition of these basic planning assumptions (and most sailors adhere to them whether they have ever consciously phrased them or not) may give some clues to the sailor's behavior even in situations only remotely related to planning for war. In no sense are they formal or official. They are just an attempt to condense some fairly general tacit understandings.

The first assumption is that *the aim of war is some measure of control over the enemy.* By control, in this broadest sense, we mean in effect the creation of conditions more favorable to us than would have existed had we not gone to war, a control over the enemy sufficient to re-settle him, after the fighting, into some acceptable status in whatever may be the postwar scheme of the world. The key in this rather loose statement is the idea that control, in one fashion or another, is the distant strategic aim. Our war aim is not necessarily met with defeat of the enemy's armed forces. It may not even be met by his governmental collapse or surrender. And it is certainly not met if all the enemy citizens (and most of our own) are the victims of a thermonuclear double-suicide. A primary and central problem in warfare is the sensing of what kinds and degrees of control may result from this or that action in this or that situation. And one can reasonably doubt that we can be very specific about it before an actual situation is at hand to be weighed in judgment. A type and intensity of control, direct or indirect, that may be excellent for one situation may be quite inapplicable in another. But the idea of control, as an aim, does markedly widen the horizons open to us in our thoughts and planning for war.

There are several methods by which control may be sought, either at sea or on the land. Some degree of military control may be achieved by destruction, the direct destruction of enemy strength, the men, the weapons, and the component parts of the physical supporting structure leading from the weapons all the way back through the communications to the basic raw materials. This is an area with which most of the world by now is thoroughly familiar.

A sort of corollary or offshoot of this might be called control by immobilization or paralysis . . . and it is mentioned here because it may be an area worth considerably more thought than has been given it in the recent past.

A more positive degree of control and a more viable one, though a more difficult one to attain, may be had by occupation, *i.e.*, the physical occupation of an area or of selected governing focal points.

A control of sorts may be exercised by the announced or tacit threat of destruction, or perhaps by the threat of occupation. While control-by-threat is variable and sometimes uncertain both in degree and its durability, it is often politically and militarily the most advisable method of applying force.

There are, of course, the more indirect forms of control by economic, political, social, and psychological pressures, all of which, by the way, have consistently played an important role in the application of maritime strategies.

The second basic assumption for war planning is that *we can not with certainty predict the complete pattern of the war for which we prepare ourselves.* The time, the place, the scope, the intensity, the course, and the general tenor of a next war are all dim and uncertain matters. Aggressors can fix the initial time and place, and we may not see it until late in its making. Who saw well ahead to Guadalcanal, or Korea, or the Suez? It is the possibility of these situations that we must keep in mind, and the more astute and inclusive is our planning the better can we manage them when they do appear.

When we accept this admittedly oversimplified premise that we can not with certainty forecast the pattern of war, nor its time, nor its place, nor its characteristics, then we arrive at the conclusion that the primary requisite in peacetime planning is more than a single rigid plan for war. Our first requirement is for a planning concept that covers a spectrum of possibilities, for the broadest possible conceptual span embracing in both time and character any military-force situation which might arise. Then, after we have in mind a full span of concept, we can take up specific situations for one of two reasons. The first is for the derivation of logistic and material needs; and the second is to meet circumstances in which the probability or the hazard (either or both of them) is so clearly marked that specific and realistic plans can in fact be drawn on such a basis. We have one such specific situation now in Europe, and it is met by the NATO arrangement. We have another of a different sort in the Middle East, and the nation's response to that one is not yet clear at this writing.

Recent game theories have sharpened one aspect of this. The player who employs only one rigid strategy runs a great risk simply because his opponent soon detects the single strategy and counters it. The requirement is for strategies of depth and breadth, flexible and adaptable, which by intent and by design can be applied to unforeseen situations. Planning for this kind of relative uncertainty is not as dangerous as it might

153

seem; there is, after all, some order in military affairs. But planning for certitude is the greatest of all military mistakes, as military history demonstrates all too vividly. This point is noted here to indicate that we need not remain always within whatever may be the prevalent opinion of the moment.

The field is wide open.

Leaving this slippery business of assumptions, we come to the maritime concept of strategy, which is a much more inclusive matter than the specific subject of naval warfare. The sailor's view of strategy presupposes a situation in which maritime communications can have an effect on warfare. The United States, connected to the rest of the world by all its oceans, is in a situation where maritime communications do in fact have great influence on the national conduct and the national policy. It is not necessary here to go into our dependence on ocean transportation as a critical feature of our economy. And hardly more so to comment that our world-wide commitments and our foreign policies themselves, all around the world, are founded on two and only two common factors. One of these is a sort of loose harmony of political aims (individualism as opposed to statism in the broadest sense), and the other is the common link of maritime communications. The most important of our current political alignments actually takes its name from the common linkage of the North Atlantic maritime communications system.

This should be enough, on behalf of the sailor, to establish that the United States is legitimately concerned with matters maritime in its strategy. He does not claim that our national interest is exclusively maritime by any means, but he does insist that maritime interests and the maritime elements be considered among the fundamental factors in any total assessment.

In the maritime pattern of thought, the sailor sees his tasks falling into two major fields, and while they are separated here simply for convenience in this discussion, one should recognize that in practice they are so closely interwoven that it is hard to tell where one stops and the other starts.

One half of the task is the establishment of control of the sea which, of course, includes the depths of its waters and the air above it. The other half is the exploitation of that control of the sea toward extension of control from the sea onto the land.

Control of the sea is a very terse phrase for a very fluid and dynamic and many-faceted series of situations. It is seldom absolute and it seldom need be. In a great many situations, a potential control of the sea is all that need be exercised. We are doing that today, all around the world. Without potential control, the NATO and the SEATO and all our other formal and informal organizations would at once collapse. Limited degrees of control may suffice, or local controls. We need not go further than to indicate that control of the sea is a situational problem that we adapt to whatever may be the requirements of the moment.

The business of setting up and holding and enjoying control of the sea is an early and potent step in establishing control over the enemy. It sets the scene of war closer to his territory, not ours, and it gives us the strategic choice of the next move. It makes it more readily a case of "what shall we do?" instead of "what do we think he will do?" When we own the world's maritime communication system, the strategic freedom of choice is ours more than his.

Then there is the extension of control from the sea onto the land—control sought in part by destruction, in part perhaps by paralysis, in part by injection of soldiery when and where it serves our needs. In general, our control of the seas imposes on the enemy a very real limitation on his freedom of action and this pervasive stifling operates quietly but continuously to project our control onto the land. The seas are to him a barrier rather than an avenue. The restrictions that bind him, militarily, economically, politically, psychologically, are not less real because they are subtle and elusive. Every U.S. soldier in Europe or in the Far East today is an extension of this nation's maritime power. Every one of our air bases outside our continent is an extension of our nation's control at sea toward the establishment of control over the enemy.

From these two, control of the sea and its exploitation, come the missions of the Navy. They are clear and direct. These are the sailor's reason for his being:

The Navy will defend the United States from attack across the seas.

The Navy will seek out and destroy enemy naval forces, shipping, bases, and supporting activities.

The Navy will deny to the enemy his use of the seas.

The Navy will control the vital sea areas, the narrow seas, the ocean approaches, the Mediterranean, the China seas, and our own adjacent waters.

And the Navy will exploit our general sea supremacy to project, protect, and sustain the combined military and civilian powers of the United States across the seas.

Against this background, then, we approach the full span of war contingencies and the part the Navy must play in any war, large or small, limited or unlimited, local or general, nuclear or non-nuclear.

It should be amply clear by now that the United States has no intention of starting any wars. So that leaves two alternatives. First, a war could be deliberately initiated against the United States by an enemy. If he did start a war, he would hardly do so in expectation of his own early defeat. It might be by a sudden blow (which is the way wars often start), or it might be at the culmination of a period of heightened tension with attendant warning of his preparation. In either event, he would have some sort of plan which would give, as he saw it, promise of a fairly sure victory over us.

The other way it might start would be from a gradual and unwanted expansion of a local conflict because of increasing friction and expanding tension in some local area. A good melee in the Middle East, for instance, might very well be expanded by growing intransigence to include Europe, and then we would probably be well into it.

No matter how it might start, the operational stages of almost any kind of war might be classified by the sailor in this fashion:

Defense of the United States
Maintenance of our world wide communications
Stabilization of the war
Taking control of the pattern of war
Establishment of control over the enemy.

This is not quite the orthodox method of breaking down a war for analysis, and so a little explanation here may be in order.

The first of these, defense of the United States, is fairly clearcut. As far as the sailor is concerned, it is the indisputable task of the Navy to defend the United States from attack across the seas, be it by submarine, or by missile, or by aircraft, or by ship. By standing ready between the United States and any enemy, it is the duty of the Navy to ensure that a war is fought overseas instead of over Chicago.

The second, the maintenance of world-wide communications, means control and use of the seas. The sailor feels that this is critical. Unless we do this, the ground forces have had it, and the deployed Air Forces have had it, and our allies are all done, and we are all in a truly serious situation. If we do not have a control of the sea adequate to deliver food to Europe and fuel to the overseas pipe-lines and ammunition to the troops abroad, then things will be black indeed.

The third item listed was stabilization of the war. This is worth a moment of comment. We noted earlier that the United States has no intention of starting the war. If an enemy starts it, he will, of course, do so on terms that are favorable to him.

157

No one is so silly as to start a war any other way. Therefore we can expect a fair measure of initial success by whoever may be the enemy. We are, one way or another, probably going to get our ears pinned back in the beginning. Our early task, then, is to bring into being some sort of a stabilized situation where we can get our breath and flex our own muscles. We will have to reinforce and shuffle our forces to accommodate to his initial moves, hold what we can, and whittle down his forces until we get some kind of dynamic balance in this total sum of the fighting.

Then, unless we are willing to fight the war through on his terms (as we did, for instance, in World War I), we will have to take control of the pattern of the war and shift it to a character or locale of our own choosing, some type of war in which we are strong and in which, preferably, he is weak.

The process of deliberately changing the character or the scene of the war is a matter that has not been consciously thought through as thoroughly as it deserves. It requires a far more searching study than can be covered in so short a space as this. In World War I, the entire war was fought by the Allies along the pattern initially set by the Germans. Once World War II was more or less stabilized, the Allies changed the character of the war both in Europe and in the Pacific. In Europe, once the Western forces were driven off the continent, the centers of pressure were moved in succession to North Africa, to Italy, and then back to France. The center of air interest was moved from the channel to Germany itself.

In the Pacific, the Japanese had their initial interest in the southern islands. The war there was finally stabilized by actions at Midway and in the South Pacific, and then we took charge and shifted the main scene of that war at our will to the Central Pacific and eventually to the Empire itself. It made a far easier problem than it would have been had we kept to the Japanese plan and tried to work back over their chosen routes from, let us say, Singapore and New Guinea through Indonesia and Southeast Asia.

In Korea, we were having the devil's own job in the south until the scene and the entire character of the war were shifted by the move to Inchon and Seoul. Later in that war, incidentally, the intense desire of a goodly number of the participants to shift the scene and character of the air war was not granted for reasons outside our interest in this discussion. There is no need to speculate on what the effect might have been; there are strong opinions on both sides of that matter.

These are cited to illustrate a concept that is a little difficult to describe in precise terms. The contestant who controls the pattern of the war has an inestimable advantage. He can, in great measure, call the tune and make the opponent dance to it.

Let us assume for illustration that the main feature of the war, as an enemy might start it, is a drive to conquer Western Europe. If he wants this, he will of course have to attempt many other tasks, such as denial to us of our sea communications and destruction of the United States industrial and military support, but these latter would be means to his end of conquering Western Europe.

Then let us assume that somehow or other we have managed to stabilize the war, holding somewhere in Europe, keeping our sea lanes sufficiently clear for use, keeping the United States militarily and economically functioning under whatever may be the damage from the air. Then how do we go on, how do we aim to take control over the enemy?

One school of thought feels that a sufficient degree of control can be had by destruction, massive and near-total destruction of the enemy war-machine. Since we have postulated that this war does, somehow, start, then we must recognize that an enemy will have figured either that he can absorb our punishment, fend it off, or deliver more than he gets. The point to be made is that there is a possibility that destruction alone will not force him to quit. Knowing what he would of his own strength and of ours, we cannot assume that he would start a war in the face of certain defeat. This means hard fighting ahead. Even after a nuclear exchange, tough men will fight on. Once we have stabilized the war, we may have to do something more than try to impose our control by destruction alone. We may well need to inject troops—the classical man on the scene with a gun—to exercise the durable and continuing control that can rarely be had in any other way.

There are three ways to do this. One is to push the enemy armies all the way back where they came from, another is to fly the troops in, and the third is to sail them in. It is a long and dreary walk across an entire continent, and one can only hope that the soldiers don't choose to try that one. The other two ways offer considerable promise. Flying them in in limited numbers might be quicker, and it offers more choice of destination, but it is far more demanding and difficult in terms of continued support. The logistic problems for a force of any appreciable size are enormous. Injection from the sea offers less latitude in terms of initial destination, but it is a far more manageable proposition both in the strengths of the forces which can be injected and in the continuing support after they get there.

Fortunately, since we have the maritime strength, we can use whatever waters may lead most conveniently to some of the more sensitive areas. That ability we should exploit. Keep in mind, in this respect, that of all the techniques and methods of warfare, there is only one in which any nation holds a monopoly. This is the attack from the sea. No other nation in the world has this great potential to any significant degree. We should exploit it to the fullest. And further, we should combine it with other types of pressures leading toward control, some of them only remotely military and which appear as political, social or economic measures.

All of these are directly involved in the business of waging war to gain some measure of control over an enemy. The peculiar versatility of naval power, in peace or war, serves to keep the sailor constantly aware of the wide range of pressures available in the national power structure.

So, one base of the sailor's planning process is a tacit appreciation that the aim of war is not limited to any particular military or naval accomplishment, rather, that all our military actions, and our non-military actions as well, must contribute to eventual control over the enemy.

This, to go back to the beginning, is really the aim of war. The other of the two basic assumptions noted that the full shape and course of war were not predictable with certainty.

In this connection, it is interesting to note that our present national attitude toward war seems to lean rather heavily on the expectation of control by destruction and the resultant immobilization. Indeed, the newly appointed Supreme Allied Commander in Europe made this quite clear in one of his first public announcements.

But along with this we have also at hand the not irrational supposition that no enemy would let himself get into a war unless he thought he could win it. So there does appear some possibility, through some combination of defense or mutual air exhaustion or mutual recognition of radiological hazard or something not now foreseen, that we might not attain an adequate control through our nuclear destruction effort alone.

In whatever case may be taken under study, it is the nation with the maritime strength that has the freedom of action. The maritime power need *not* irrevocably commit itself to any single course of action. Once the war is stabilized, it can pick and choose its opportunities. It is the nation with the maritime strength which is in the best position to control the

161

course of war, to select the strategic pattern of the war, to fit its strength to whatever may be the requirements as the war progresses, and to impose on any enemy whatever kind and degree of control may be needed to meet the nation's aims.

Perhaps this indicates a little of why sailors think the way they do. Why, for instance, they design and plan the Navy as a versatile and multi-purpose instrument of power, designed to defend the United States and to respond to the needs of national policy in whatever situation may develop.

The conclusion that the sailor has not always been able to explain too clearly is that, no matter what single situation is taken up for discussion be it great or small, nuclear or non-nuclear, it is not adequate to assess the usefulness of naval power only in terms of that one situation. The collateral values in other situations must be brought into the equation to arrive at a valid judgment.

In closing, though, one point should be made quite clear. Although the sailor is no less, and one can hope no more, partisan than any other military man, no sailor is so naive as to suppose that the Navy alone is going to sail out and win all our wars. But what he can do is fix it so the soldier's strength and the airman's strength and the sailor's strength as well as the political, economic, and social strengths of this country can be applied in combinations as needed to defend the United States and to establish whatever kind and degree of control the United States may need.

That is why the sailor asks, when his nation considers these matters, that the nation keep in mind that the maritime strategies are the one field in which the United States has an inherent advantage over any enemy. The sailor hopes the nation, if it is ever forced to war, will take advantage of that, use it, and exploit it for all it is worth. It will save time, and it will save effort, and when all the figures are totalled up, it will probably save a good many lives.

INDEX

Abbas, Abbu, 102 fn
Afghanistan, 86
aggressor, 74–76, 100
air warfare, 26, 129, 137, 139, 140–41, 141–43; theory of, 33, 36–41, 63, 84, 86, 87, 99, 124–25; limitations of theory, 56–58
Albion, Robert G., xxiii
Alexander the Great, 76
Algeria, 53
American Sail Training Association, xxxi
amphibious warfare, 35
Anglo-Dutch wars, 128
Argentine Naval War College, xxxiv
Armada, 128
arms, 138–40
Arnold, General H. H., 37
Asiatic Fleet (U.S.), xi–xiii
Atlantic Fleet (U.S.), xviii, xxx
Australian Naval Institute, xxxiv

Baldwin, Hanson, xxxii
Baltic Sea, 132, 145

Baxter, James Phinney, xxiii
Beaufre, General André, xxxiii, 59 fn
blockade, 125
Bookman, Lieut. (j.g.) Robert E., xvi
budget, defense, 64
Burdick, Eugene, xxiii, xxiv, 91, 95 fn
Burke, Commodore Arleigh, xix

Carney, Admiral Robert B., xiii
Castro, Fidel, 49, 107
center of gravity, 77–88, 93, 97, 98, 105, 106, 133
Churchill, Winston, 8, 44, 54, 76
CIC, x, xv–xviii
civilians and study of war, 1–2, 66
Civil War (U.S.), 25, 79–80, 120
Clausewitz, Carl von, 8, 10, 17, 44–45; limitations of theory, 54–55, 59, 63, 67–69

163

Cole, Rear Admiral William M.,
  xiv
Combat Information Center,
  see CIC
commerce protection, 125,
  126, 154–55
Concorde aircraft, 114
conservator, 74–76, 100
continental warfare, 27,
  41–48, 124, 129, 137, 139
Conolly, Admiral Richard L.,
  xx–xxiii
control, as aim of warfare,
  xxvi, 34, 36, 41, 66–70,
  77–78, 87–89, 93, 97, 101,
  103, 105, 106, 115, 151–52
control of the sea, 125–27,
  154–55, 161
Corbett, Sir Julian, 10, 10 fn,
  13, 33–34
cost-effectiveness, 87, 88
Cuba, 53, 68, 92
culture, xii, xxiv, 2, 62, 70; *see
  also* strategy, as a social
  discipline
cumulative strategies, xxv,
  22–27, 80–81, 99, 101–2,
  117–21

Dardanelles, 80–81
Day, Comdr. Edward, xvi
defensive, 17–18, 74–76
Delaney, Professor Robert F.,
  104, 104 fn, 105
delousing operations, xix
Dennison, Admiral Robert L.,
  xxix
destruction and its relationship

to control, 88–89, 99, 101,
  115, 138–39, 143–44, 152,
  159–60
DEW line, 113–14
Deyo, Rear Admiral M. L.,
  xviii
Dienbienphu, 47
diplomacy, xi–xii, 88–89
Douhet, Giulio, 36–41, 58

Earle, Professor Edward M.,
  xxiii
Eccles, Rear Admiral Henry E.,
  xxiv; comment on *Military
  Strategy*, xxxii–xxxiii
economics, 8, 128, 129, 154,
  159
Eisenhower, General Dwight, 1,
  44, 54–55
equilibrium in war, 75–76, 79,
  82, 83; *see also* stabilization
ergonomics, x, xx
Espiritu Santo, xviii
explosives in war, 137–39

Federal Shipbuilding and Dry
  Dock Co., *see* Kearney, N.J.
Ford, Henry, 8

game theory, 71, 153
geography, 80; *see also* terrain
Giap, General Vo Nguyen, 49,
  52–54, 106–8
Gorshkov, Admiral Sergei,
  xxx–xxxi
Grant, General U. S., 79
Greece, 145
Greenwood Press, xxxiv

ABOUT THE EDITOR

John B. Hattendorf has been the Ernest J. King Professor of Maritime History at the Naval War College since 1983. He is the senior editor of the Classics of Sea Power series.

After receiving his bachelor's degree in history from Kenyon College in 1964, Hattendorf served at sea in both Atlantic and Pacific Fleet destroyers, seeing combat action in Vietnam. Later he served ashore at the Naval Historical Center in Washington and on the staff of the Naval War College. After leaving active duty, he obtained a master's degree in history at Brown University and went on to obtain his doctorate at the University of Oxford in England.

The editor of a number of volumes of naval documents as well as articles on naval history and strategy, he has most recently written *England in the War of the Spanish Succession* and edited, with Robert S. Jordan, *Maritime Strategy and the Balance of Power: Britain and America in the 20th Century.*

ISBN 0-87021-362-8